THE NEUTRON BOMB CONTROVERSY

Foreign Policy Issues
A Foreign Policy Research Institute Series

Series Editor
NILS H. WESSELL

Managing Editor
CHARLES B. PURRENHAGE

THE NEUTRON BOMB CONTROVERSY

A Study in Alliance Politics

Sherri L. Wasserman

PRAEGER SPECIAL STUDIES • PRAEGER SCIENTIFIC

Library of Congress Cataloging in Publication Data

Wasserman, Sherri L.

  The neutron bomb controversy.
  "Submitted to an Interdisciplinary Committee on
International Relations of Amherst College in partial
fulfillment of the requirements for the degree of
Bachelor of Arts with honors--Professors Theodore Greene,
William Taubman, and Joel Wolfe, April 28, 1981."
    Bibliography: p.
    Includes index.
    1. North Atlantic Treaty Organization. 2. United
    States--Military policy. 3. Neutron bomb. I. Title.
UA646.3.W37 1983   355'.031'091821   83-6797
ISBN 0-03-064154-3

For my parents, *George* and *Renate Wasserman*

Published in 1983 by Praeger Publishers
CBS Educational and Professional Publishing
a Division of CBS Inc.
521 Fifth Avenue, New York, NY 10175 USA

© Sherri L. Wasserman

3456789 052 987654321
Printed in the United States of America
on acid-free paper

Foreword

This volume is another in the Foreign Policy Research Institute's book series, *Foreign Policy Issues*. The series includes both collectively and individually authored works on contemporary international relations. The series provides a publication outlet for work by researchers at the Foreign Policy Research Institute and by other authors, such as Sherri Wasserman, in the academic and "policy" communities.

Like the question of deploying Pershing II and ground–launched cruise missiles in Europe, the enhanced radiation warhead (ERW) acquired a political significance transcending its military purpose. Sherri Wasserman points out that on the level of military doctrine the disagreement over deployment of "the neutron bomb" has similarly turned on the advisability of NATO's preparing to fight a limited nuclear war both as a deterrent to Warsaw Pact aggression and as a means of defense. The military rationale behind deployment of ERWs was, and is, to minimize "collateral damage" to Western Europe's civilian infrastructure while destroying the Warsaw Pact's military personnel, thereby enhancing the credibility of the NATO deterrent.

But as this study indicates, the process of decision making both between governments and within governments sometimes exerts a decisive impact on the decision itself. Relying on Richard Neustadt's framework for understanding alliance politics, the author examines the role of domestic political factors and competing bureaucratic interests in President Carter's 1978 decision to postpone production of ERWs followed by President Reagan's decision to produce (but not necessarily deploy) the warhead.

Most disturbingly, the author concludes that while the Reagan administration learned from the mistakes of its predecessor that consistent U.S. leadership is needed in NATO nuclear decision making, it failed to learn the more important lesson that U.S. leadership, to be successful, must address European political concerns. In the author's words, "the real lesson to be learned is that governments rarely learn lessons."

Charles E. Purrenhage and Elizabeth Dunlap ably supervised production of the volume, which began under the energetic guidance of Alan Ned Sabrosky. To them we owe a debt of gratitude.

Nils H. Wessell
Series Editor
Foreign Policy Issues
A Foreign Policy Research
Institute Study

This book is about the *politics* of the neutron bomb controversy. It is not a polemic about the military virtues and vices of enhanced radiation warheads. It is a study of the politics of decisionmaking for the procurement and deployment of nuclear weapons in Europe. As such, I hope this book imparts some sense of how individuals, bureaucracies, governments, and alliances make decisions on perhaps the most important phenomenon of this century: nuclear weapons.

My research on the neutron bomb controversy began in spring 1980. I was an undergraduate at Amherst College, taking my junior year at the London School of Economics. The course I found most challenging dealt with such topics as American and Soviet strategic thinking about nuclear deterrence, limited war, and arms control. Philip Windsor, Reader in International Relations, had an unforgetable way of making his students feel that strategic studies comprised *the* issues of our age: What is the meaning of nuclear deterrence? How many and what types of weapons are needed to maintain the security of the United States and the NATO alliance? No one right answer exists to these types of questions. Yet they raise issues that must be addressed, problems that must be solved.

So I set out to solve the mystery of the neutron bomb controversy. Why had a weapon of relatively marginal military utility created such an uproar in the Alliance? After all, NATO had deployed nuclear weapons in Europe since the 1950s, all with greater destructive capability than the enhanced radiation warhead. My search took me to the International Institute for Strategic Studies, where the extensive files and patient librarians helped me to begin piecing together the puzzle. Once the general outline of the case had been constructed, I sought clarification and insight into the decision-making process from those with first-hand knowledge of the events.

I am fortunate in having had the opportunity to discuss the events of the neutron bomb controversy with a number of individuals in London and Washington who were in some way connected with this sensitive and controversial matter. Much of what was recorded is still classified, and the public record is often misleading. Numerous interviews with both participants and observers have been indispensable to the reconstruction of events. I am grateful to all of them for their time, their candor, and their patience with a persistent student. The price paid for the privilege of first-hand knowledge is the confidentiality of sources. But as Richard Neustadt noted, "were a student

made to choose, God forbid, between the files and memories of participants, he would do well to take the latter."[1]

I am indebted to a number of individuals whose assistance has been indispensable to this study. Gregory Treverton guided me through the early stages of this project in London and cheerfully endured my many requests for advice and comment. Walter Slocombe has seen me through the entire study, from encouraging me to pursue the complexities of the neutron bomb controversy to commenting on an (almost) final draft. My advisors, T. P. Greene, William Taubman, and Joel Wolfe, have served me well throughout, patiently commenting on every chapter. I owe a special thanks to Bill Taubman for his unfailing guidance and assistance. My colleagues at Science Applications, Inc. helped to sustain my morale during the completion of this study. Finally, to my friends at Amherst for their encouragement throughout this project, I am most grateful, especially to Dan Stein, whose comfort and inspiration made all the hardships worthwhile.

---

[1] Richard E. Neustadt, *Alliance Politics* (New York: Columbia University Press, 1970), p. 7.

CONTENTS

List of Abbreviations

ABM	antiballistic missile
ACDA	Arms Control and Disarmament Agency
ACIS	Arms Control Impact Statement
ADM	atomic demolition munition
AEC	Atomic Energy Commission
AFAP	artillery fired atomic projectile
CDU/CSU	Christian Democratic Union/Christian Social Union
CRS	Congressional Research Service
CSCE	Conference on Security and Cooperation in Europe
CTB	Comprehensive Test Ban
DoD	Department of Defense
DPC	Defense Planning Committee
ERDA	Energy Research and Development Administration
ERW	enhanced radiation warhead
FDP	Free Democratic Party
FRG	Federal Republic of Germany
HLG	High Level Group (NATO)
INF	intermediate nuclear force
IRBM	intermediate range ballistic missile
JCAE	Joint Committee on Atomic Energy
JCS	Joint Chiefs of Staff
MAD	Mutual Assured Destruction
MBFR	Mutual Balanced Force Reductions
MIRV	multiple independent reentry vehicle
MLF	Multilateral Force
NAC	North Atlantic Council
NATO	North Atlantic Treaty Organization
NPG	Nuclear Planning Group (NATO)
NPT	Non-Proliferation Treaty
NSC	National Security Council
SAC	Strategic Air Command
SACEUR	Supreme Allied Commander, Europe
SALT	Strategic Arms Limitation Talks
SCC	Special Coordinating Committee
SCG	Special Consultative Group (NATO)
SPD	Social Democratic Party
TNF	theatre nuclear forces
TNW	tactical nuclear weapon
WP	Warsaw Pact

1977

June 6 An article by Walter Pincus, "Neutron Killer Warhead Buried in ERDA Budget," is published in the *Washington Post*.

  22 The Senate Appropriations Committee approves production funds for the Lance ERW, defeating 10-10 an amendment by Senator Hatfield to delete such funding.

  24 Senator Pell requests Paul Warnke, Director of the Arms Control and Disarmament Agency, to coordinate the preparation of an Arms Control Impact Statement on the Lance ERW.

  26 President Carter's press secretary, Jody Powell, says that Carter wants Congress to approve stand-by funds to produce and deploy ERWs.

July 1 Senate holds closed session to debate ERWs. In open session, the Senate votes 43-42 in favor of an amendment by Senator Stennis to delay funds for ERWs "until an Arms Control Impact Statement has been filed with Congress and the President certifies to Congress that these weapons are in the national interest."

  6 Jody Powell announces that President Carter will decide shortly after mid-August whether to recommend production of ERWs.

  11 In a letter to Senator Stennis, President Carter urges Congress to appropriate funds for the production of ERWs.

  12 In a press conference, Carter says, "I have not yet decided whether to approve the neutron bomb. I do think it ought to be one of our options, however."

  13 Arms Control Impact Statement on Lance ERW is sent to Congress. President Carter tells the Senate that although the neutron bomb would deter communists, it might have a "marginally negative" effect on the SALT talks. Senate passes, 74-19, an amendment by Senator Byrd prohibiting production of ERWs until the president certifies that production is in

the national interest, and giving Congress the authority to disapprove production of ERWs if both Houses pass a concurrent resolution to do so within 45 days of such a presidential certification. Moscow warns that the neutron bomb may create a standstill in SALT (Strategic Arms Limitation Talks) and MBFR (Mutual Balanced Force Reductions) forums.

18 Egon Bahr, Secretary General of the West German Social Democratic Party, criticizes the neutron bomb as a "symbol of mental perversity."

September   8 West German Parliament debates ERWs.

27 National Security Advisor Brzezinski meets with Chancellor Schmidt in Bonn to discuss ERWs.

Soviet Foreign Minister Gromyko calls for a UN ban on the neutron bomb in an address to the UN General Assembly.

October 11-12 NATO Defense Ministers meeting in Bari, Italy, fail to agree on ERW production and deployment.

28 Chancellor Schmidt, in London, calls for examination of ERWs in light of their relevance to arms control.

November   7 Dutch Parliament holds a debate on ERWs.

15 The West German Social Democratic Party calls on Schmidt to arrange his security and disarmament policies so that the deployment of ERWs in West Germany is not necessary.

23 Press reports indicate that the Carter administration is examining the possibility of limiting the production of ERWs in return for a Soviet pledge to limit the SS-20.

December   8-9 NATO Nuclear Planning Group meeting in Brussels fails to achieve agreement on ERWs.

23 In *Pravda* interview, Brezhnev proposes that Moscow and Washington jointly renounce production of ERWs and threatens to produce them if the United States declines his offer.

.30 Washington launches a public attack against the Soviet SS-20 to defuse Moscow's propaganda campaign against the ERW.

1978

January 23 Brezhnev sends letters to heads of European NATO countries warning that deployment of ERWs will jeopardize East-West détente.

February 1 Several members of West Germany's Social Democratic Party suggest using ERWs as a bargaining chip in MBFR talks.

23 The West German conservative opposition parties pass a unanimous resolution in favor of the deployment of ERWs. The Bonn government urges that the greatest possible effort be made to include ERWs in arms control negotiations before deployment is considered.

The Dutch government vows to try to prevent NATO's deployment of ERWs.

24 At a meeting of NATO ambassadors in Brussels, Leslie Gelb, Director of the State Department's Bureau of Politico–Military Affairs, proposes using ERWs as a bargaining chip in East-West arms control negotiations.

March 4 Dutch Defense Minister Rölof Kruisinga resigns in protest over ERWs.

8 Dutch Parliament votes 110-40 to oppose the deployment of ERWs before arms control negotiations have been held.

19 President Carter rejects a decision memorandum urging production and deployment of ERWs.

20 Washington cancels meeting of NATO's North Atlantic Council at which agreement on production and deployment of ERWs was to be announced.

30 Deputy Secretary of State Warren Christopher travels to Bonn to inform Chancellor Schmidt and Foreign Minister Genscher that Carter is inclined to cancel ERWs.

April 4 *The New York Times* reports that Carter has decided to cancel ERW production.

Senator Robert Byrd releases a letter to Carter informing him of the diminished chances for Senate ratification of SALT II if Carter cancels ERW without a Soviet *quid pro quo*. Genscher arrives in Washington to discuss ERWs with Carter.

7 Carter announces his decision to defer ERW production but says that the ultimate decision regarding incorporation of enhanced radiation features will be influenced by the degree to which the Soviet Union "shows restraint" in its conventional and nuclear arms programs and force deployments.

9 Secretary of Defense Harold Brown says ERWs were "useful militarily" but that there are "other ways to do the same thing."

12 Schmidt states that the Federal Republic would be willing to allow deployment of ERWs on German soil provided that NATO approves and the weapons are also deployed in another continental European country.

13 Schmidt rallies behind Carter's ERW decision in a speech to the Bundestag.

Introduction

On April 7, 1978 President Carter announced his decision to defer production of enhanced radiation warheads, otherwise known as the neutron bomb. This decision brought a temporary close to the heated and highly publicized debate over the production and deployment of this battlefield nuclear weapon. The decision came as a surprise to the NATO allies, who, in response to pressure from Washington, were on the verge of agreeing to deployment. The U.S. Congress had already appropriated funds for the production of ERWs. And West Germany, on whose territory the bulk of the weapons would have been stationed, had expressed willingness, albeit conditionally, to deploy them. By March 1978 the Carter administration and the NATO allies had reached agreement on a plan to produce and deploy ERWs. One objective of this study is to determine why President Carter chose to reverse his administration's course of action at the eleventh hour.

Three years later, the Reagan administration reviewed the issue and, finding President Carter's resolution unsatisfactory, announced its intention to complete development of the warhead. This decision took the form of a unilateral pronouncement on development and production; no official arrangements were made with the NATO allies to deploy the warhead in Europe. The directive called for the warheads to be stockpiled in the United States and made available for deployment to Europe if a need for them should arise. Reaction in Europe to President Reagan's decision was generally unfavorable, expressed most dramatically in the "peace" demonstrations that raged throughout Europe in autumn 1981. Thanks in part to these demonstrations, the neutron bomb has come to symbolize nuclear malaise in the Atlantic Alliance. Thus its importance as an issue to the security of the Alliance and to relations among the allies in many ways supercedes its military significance. A second objective of this study is to examine what the neutron bomb controversy, from its inception in June 1977 to its present status under the Reagan administration, reveals about American approaches to the modernization of tactical nuclear weapons and to nuclear decision making within NATO.

During the Carter administration, as much controversy centered around *how* and *by whom* the decision would be made (Should the United States make the first commitment to produce the weapons? Should West Germany make a prior commitment to deploy them?) as focused on the more central issue of whether or not ERWs are a needed improvement to NATO's military

capabilities. More recently, the Reagan administration took a different approach that adopted a two-step process: production as a unilateral U.S. decision and deployment as a separate decision to be negotiated within the Alliance. This approach implicitly rejected the previously accepted dual-track scheme in which production and deployment are simultaneously negotiated by NATO participants and the fulfillment of one component is dependent upon the other. The political consequences of President Reagan's decision will not fully surface until the United States again seeks to deploy the ERW in Europe.

Behind these political decisions lie more fundamental military issues. What role, for example, does NATO military doctrine play in determining weapons acquisition? Doctrine—a set of ideas pertaining to the purpose of weapons and forces—is thought by many to be the decisive factor in weapons acquisition. The relationship between NATO's military doctrine and the decision to propose the addition of ERWs to NATO's tactical nuclear arsenal is a major consideration of this study.

A basis for conflict existed in NATO's military doctrine. The debate centered on to what extent NATO should orient its defense posture toward the possibility of fighting a limited nuclear war. This is the fundamental dilemma surrounding all battlefield nuclear weapons. But the emotion and publicity generated by the neutron bomb exposed the unanswered questions in NATO's force posture in a new and more dramatic light. For example, by giving NATO greater potential to fight a limited nuclear war, will battlefield nuclear weapons increase deterrence, or will they increase the likelihood that NATO may actually engage in nuclear battle? NATO's "Overall Defense Concept for the Central Area," flexible response, offers little guidance on this issue; in fact, it is deliberately vague. Europe would like to interpret the doctrine as providing for the almost immediate escalation of a limited nuclear conflict to the strategic level. In this way their homelands might be spared the widespread devastation resulting from a nuclear war limited to Europe. The United States, on the other hand, would prefer to construe "flexible" as allowing for the possibility that, in the event of a Warsaw Pact attack, Europe might be adequately defended with conventional forces and, if necessary, battlefield nuclear weapons, halting the conflict before escalation becomes necessary. Because every country strives to protect its own territory, regardless of notions of collective security, NATO members have always found it expedient to leave the purposes of battlefield nuclear weapons suitably ambiguous, allowing margin for various interpretations.

Another key factor in any decision to acquire new weapons is technological innovation. What is the relationship between technology and weapons acquisition? Some believe that technological advances become a factor in weapons acquisition "only insofar as suitable doctrines are devised to govern their strategic and tactical employment."[1] Others believe that

technology itself may acquire a momentum of its own that can open up new possibilities and force decisions.[2] Technological improvements may be used to bolster the plausibility of an argument for acquiring new weapons systems and hence lead to a more intensified effort to secure the production and deployment of a particular weapon, even if there is no suitable military rationale governing the weapon's use. The influence of technological advances on the decision to produce ERWs is a vital facet of the controversy.

The development of the enhanced radiation concept was part of a broad trend in tactical nuclear weaponry toward the elimination of large-scale destruction from the use of nuclear weapons. Seen in the context of this general movement toward so-called clean nuclear weaponry, ERWs were just another application of this technological trend. Numerous attempts since the late 1950s to incorporate enhanced radiation technology into viable weapons systems had failed owing to controversy over its military utility and to a lack of interest by politicians and high-level civilian military officials. By the mid-1970s, however, the program for modernizing tactical nuclear weapons provided the momentum for the fruition of earlier efforts by the scientific and military communities to apply the enhanced radiation concept to a viable weapons system. The scientists and military services who lobbied for the weapon couched their arguments in purely technical, military terms; they were not responsible for conducting an analysis of the political implications of new weaponry. Thus the technology provided an opportunity for these groups to seek a decision on the production of ERWs.

Once there is a choice to be made, the *process* of decision almost inevitably has a tremendous impact on the decision itself. A decision to modify NATO's defense posture has at least two distinct but not operationally separate components—production and deployment—in which the constraints imposed by the first factor weigh heavily on the outcome of the second. The normal weapons acquisition process for an American–produced, NATO-Europe-deployed capability is as follows: First the American government reaches a decision to produce a new weapon by presidential approval and congressional appropriation of funds, then NATO governments arrive at a joint decision to deploy the weapon through bilateral negotiations and consultations within the Alliance. But the ERW debacle was a deviation from the normal process of decision making within NATO. The American and West European governments, particularly the West German government, did not agree on the political and procedural process through which ERWs should be produced and deployed. The Carter administration thought that an American decision to produce ERWs should follow a firm commitment from the allies to deploy the weapons. Allied governments, however, believed that the American decision to manufacture ERWs should precede NATO discussions on deployment in Europe.

To the American government, production and deployment were inextricably linked: If the chief executive was to urge Congress to appropriate

funds for the production of ERWs, then Congress not unreasonably assumed deployment should be the logical outcome. But the new president did not want to risk contradicting his commitments to disarmament and nonproliferation by unilaterally ordering production of a weapon he was not even sure the allies would deploy. He thought the Alliance should arrive at a joint decision by "consensus." The federal bureaucracies each saw slightly different faces of the issue: for the State Department, maintaining good ties with the allies was most important; for the Defense Department and the Joint Chiefs of Staff, fulfilling their alleged requirement for this warhead was preeminent; for the Arms Control and Disarmament Agency (ACDA), assessing the weapon's impact on on-going arms control negotiations was the first priority; for the National Security Council, coordinating the interests of all the bureaucracies involved with the views of the president and organizing a political strategy for allied agreement were the major concerns. The participants were influenced to a large extent by the press and the way in which it presented the issues. The neutron bomb did not become a political issue in the United States until the press brought the weapon to the public's attention. In short, each American participant responded to events according to the pressures he perceived on his interests at home.

The outcome of decision making *between* governments depends on the process of decision making *within* governments. Richard Neustadt defines alliance politics as the *inter*allied outcomes produced by the interaction of *intra*governmental games.[3] What happens when two or more governments try to resolve a common problem depends on how the domestic political considerations and bureaucratic interests of each government are perceived abroad and how this perception is applied to events at home. To understand the impact of a foreign policy decision on another government the decision maker must focus on the processes internal to the foreign government. Writing about Anglo-American relations during the Suez and Skybolt crises, Neustadt states:

> Players on the one side failed to understand the stakes of players on the other. They failed to do so because they misread the interests which the other men pursued. They misread interests because they misunderstood, to some degree, the precise nature of the game in which the others were engaged: its position, or its channels, or its history.[4]

Such is the nature of the governments involved in the neutron bomb controversy.

The constraints within each government that influence the decision making process take the form of domestic and bureaucratic politics. Domestic politics refer to pressures *outside* the executive branch that impinge on the foreign policy process. The U.S. Congress, for example, had

considerable influence on the administration's approach to ERWs by exercising its budgetary powers. Bureaucratic politics refer to political pressures from *within* the executive branch. The conventional wisdom is that participants determine their interests in and positions on a particular issue by a process of rational choice: listing and prioritizing a series of goals and objectives, considering the cost and benefits of different alternatives, searching for additional information to reduce uncertainty, and choosing among options that will assure the most favorable combination of maximized benefits and reduced uncertainty.[5] In reality, however, participants' decisions depend more on their analysis of the intragovernmental game and on their position within their particular organization than on objective criteria. The decisions that result from the interaction of participants with various and often divergent interests on an issue and different amounts of power to influence the outcome seldom reflect a single, coherent, or consistent set of calculations about the national interest. This process of decision making forms the framework for analysis of the neutron bomb controversy.

In Europe as well as in the United States, responses to external events had much to do with domestic constraints. European heads of government not unreasonably insisted that they could not be expected to persuade their legislatures and their publics to endorse the deployment of a weapon that had not yet been given full backing by the American president. In West Germany, where the domestic political constraints on the government were the most severe, the commitment to deploy ERWs was also the most crucial to allied agreement; as the principal battlefield of an attack by Warsaw Pact forces, West Germany was not only the linchpin of American decision but also the preeminent influence on the position of other NATO allies. Chancellor Schmidt could not risk defections from his party by supporting deployment of a weapon that the United States would not fully endorse. Intensive Soviet propaganda made all the European allies, especially West Germany, reluctant to support a weapon whose deployment might have adverse consequences for their much-cherished policy of détente. And so, because governments were not fully aware of the others' internal constraints, the conflict was continually fueled by misperception, poor communications, and false expectations.

This study is organized around three key elements in Alliance nuclear relations: military doctrine, technology, and the decision making process.

Chapter 1 examines the dilemma in NATO's military doctrine. Chapter 2 considers the technological constraints on and incentives for the development of ERWs. The next four chapters deal with the events of the controversy from June 1977 to April 1978, concentrating on the process by which the participants—individuals, organizations, governments, and allies—attempted to reach a decision on the production and deployment of ERWs. Chapter 7 presents five conclusions drawn from this study and compares the approaches of the Carter and Reagan administrations in light of those conclusions.

NOTES

1. I. B. Holley, "The Evolution of Operations Research and Its Impact on the Military Establishment: The Air Force Experience," in *Science, Technology and Warfare. Proceedings of the Third History Symposium*, U.S. Air Force Academy, ed. Monte D. Wight and Lawrence J. Paszek, (Washington, D.C.: 1969), p. 89.

2. Morton H. Halperin, *Bureaucratic Politics and Foreign Policy* (Washington, D.C.: The Brookings Institution, 1974), p. 102.

3. Richard E. Neustadt, *Alliance Politics* (New York: Columbia University Press, 1970), p. 7.

4. Ibid., p. 115.

5. See, for example, Thomas C. Schelling, *The Strategy of Conflict* (Cambridge, Mass.: Harvard University Press, 1960); and "Model I" in Graham T. Allison, *Essence of Decision: Explaining the Cuban Missile Crisis* (Boston: Little, Brown, 1971).

1

TNWs in Alliance Strategy: NATO's Doctrinal Dilemma

This chapter establishes the context for the ERW controversy as derived from American and NATO military doctrine. The heart of the matter is that the military doctrine that presumably governs NATO's acquisition and employment of tactical nuclear weapons (TNWs) is deliberately so vague that the doctrinal implications of ERWs were not realized until the weapon became the object of public scrutiny. The doctrinal implications are important because they reveal a fundamental difference of interests in TNWs between the United States and Europe.

The first task is to place ERWs within the broad classifications of nuclear weapons. ERWs fall into a category known as tactical nuclear weapons, as distinct from strategic nuclear weapons. While the two categories can be differentiated either by technical characteristics, such as range or yield, or by the uses of the weapons, such as types of targets, the classifications are not mutually exclusive.

The problem with precise definition is paralleled in the ambiguity of NATO's military doctrine. The ambiguity stems from interallied disagreement over the role of nuclear weapons in Europe, specifically whether battlefield nuclear weapons are to be used for defense as well as deterrence. Deterrence is primarily a psychological means of preventing war, whereas defense is the combative means of mitigating losses should deterrence fail.

Disagreement over deterrence and defense reflects a fundamental difference of interests between the United States and Europe. In the 1950s and 1960s, the United States defined the primary role of TNWs in Europe in terms of deterrence only; yet owing to changes in the strategic environment and to the

availability of new technologies, in the 1970s the United States began trying to develop rationales by which TNWs would provide effective defense as well as deterrence. This posed severe problems for Europe, which would have to entertain the notion of fighting a nuclear war on its territory if TNWs were to serve the purpose of defense. Disagreement over deterrence and defense in the late 1960s was overcome by leaving the role of TNWs ambiguous in NATO's overall military doctrine, Flexible Response. With respect to NATO's nuclear force posture, the major requirement of doctrine has been a configuration that is acceptable to all the major interests within the Alliance.

Since this difference of interests between the United States and Europe has seemed quite incapable of analytical resolution, when the Nixon administration embarked on a TNW modernization program, little attention was given to the doctrinal implications of the new weapons. Discussion in NATO avoided doctrinal issues largely because neither side wanted to upset the fragile consensus that existed only on the actual existence of TNWs in Europe, not on their role in nuclear employment planning. Thus the ERW controversy opened a Pandora's box of unresolved and perhaps irreconcilable doctrinal issues, the principal one being that if nuclear weapons are intended for the defense of Western Europe, then NATO must not only consider the possibility of but also actively plan for fighting a limited nuclear war.

The first problem with ERWs is their definition. Nuclear weapons have traditionally been divided into two broad categories: strategic nuclear weapons and tactical nuclear weapons. In 1977 ERWs were included as one feature in the modernization of artillery-fired atomic projectiles, a mobile atomic cannon, and of the Lance surface-to-surface missile. Both are antitank weapons for use in the immediate combat area and thus fall into the category known variously battlefield, short-range, or tactical nuclear weapons. Strategic nuclear weapons are generally understood to be weapons having the capability to strike targets in the homelands of the two superpowers, hence the term "intercontinental." In general, TNWs are designed to support ground forces in a particular "theater," such as Europe or Asia. The layman might reasonably infer that TNWs are a distinct category of nuclear weapons, that their destructive power and range is less than that of strategic nuclear weapons. In reality, the distinction is not nearly so simple.

No precise definition of TNWs is readily available. In NATO's early years, TNWs were generally associated with short-range weapons of relatively low explosive power, deployed on or near the battlefield, to be used only for striking military targets in the combat area. But in the almost 30 years that NATO has had TNWs, their designs and intended roles have increased enormously, making any attempt at precise definition a difficult task. An exchange between Senator Stuart Symington and Army Chief of Staff Creighton Abrams in 1973 reflects these difficulties:

Senator Symington: So what is a tactical weapon and what is a strategic weapon? I am interested in your thoughts on that and this subject in general.

General Abrams: Senator, first of all, I think both of us know that no one can say today . . . with all that we know, and all we think we know. . . .[1]

Definition of TNWs is usually attempted by comparison with strategic nuclear weapons. There are several approaches to this type of comparative definition. One is the use of inherent military capabilities to distinguish TNWs from strategic nuclear weapons. Such criteria include yield of the weapon, its range, location of the delivery system, and location of the target.

The problem with these criteria is that the categories of nuclear weapons overlaps. Implicit in classification by yield is an attempt to define as tactical those weapons that generate the least amount of collateral damage commensurate with the destruction of military targets. (Collateral damage is weapon-related destruction not dictated by the military objective of that weapon's use. It usually refers to undesirable civilian damage.) Many U.S. weapons designated as tactical possess yields far too large to permit meaningful discrimination between civilian and military targets in highly industrialized and heavily populated Central Europe. This overlap in yields blurs the distinction between TNWs and strategic nuclear weapons based on destructive potential.

Classification by yield and classification by range can produce different definitions. For example, a one-kiloton nuclear warhead, considered tactical by the yield approach, could be construed as strategic if it can be delivered on a target within the Soviet Union: Even a limited nuclear strike on Soviet territory would almost certainly provoke a strategic riposte by the USSR. The problem with classification by range is that many weapons that NATO designates for theater use only are capable of striking Soviet territory and of inflicting damage similar to that of a strategic nuclear weapons.

An approach that gained considerable support in the United States in the late 1970s is definition by the concept of tactical versus strategic *uses* of nuclear weapons, focusing on types of designated targets rather than on the inherent military capabilities of the weapons themselves. A tactical use of nuclear weapons would thus be the employment of nuclear weapons of any size against military targets directly supporting the enemy's ground forces, wherever these targets are located. Often ignored is the fact that a weapon that might be tactical for one country would be unavoidably strategic for another. Use by the United States of TNWs based on West German soil, for example, even though it did not provoke a strategic exchange between the United States and the USSR, would nevertheless be of strategic significance to West Germany. Even American strategists cannot agree on a valid distinction between the tactical and strategic uses of nuclear weapons. During the 1977 congressional debate on ERWs, Senator Mark Hatfield cited an editorial from the Washington *Star* that sheds some light on this issue:

> If the neutron warhead is thought to be a genuinely tactical or battlefield scaled nuclear weapon, it will be the first such weapon to qualify unambiguously. No strategist that we know of, from Dr. Kissinger on, has convincingly shown that a reliable distinction is to be drawn between tactical and strategic nuclear weapons.[2]

In 1978 the United States tried to define TNWs by emphasizing the doctrine governing their use: "Theater nuclear forces provide the link between conventional and strategic forces, both for deterrent purposes and militarily."[3] But what exactly are the principles governing this "linkage" between conventional and strategic forces provided by TNWs? As we shall see, the doctrine is perhaps more ambiguous than the weapons themselves.

Alliance doctrine must simultaneously satisfy the strategic objectives and domestic constraints of all Alliance members, even when their interests diverge or conflict. Each time the Alliance attempts to revise or further refine NATO's military doctrine, it runs the risk of unraveling the fabric of mutual confidence that binds its members together. The danger is even greater when the threat that the Alliance is designed to counter is perceived to decline.

The military doctrine for TNW employment was obscure in the 1970s because NATO members found their increasing divergence of interests in TNWs too disruptive to be settled by analytical means. This divergence of interests resulted from the decreasing deterrent value of strategic nuclear weapons and the subsequent attempt by the United States to design TNWs that could fill this gap. As the Soviet Union began to match the United States in strategic nuclear capabilities, the credibility of America's threat to risk all-out nuclear war to defend Europe began to diminish. In the 1950s and 1960s the United States interpreted the role of TNWs in Europe principally as a deterrent; yet owing to changes in the strategic environment, most notably Soviet advances in strategic nuclear weaponry, and to the availability of new technologies, in the late 1960s and early 1970s the United States began to move away from a deterrent-only definition of TNWs.

To understand this trend in American military doctrine, the distinction between the concepts of deterrence and defense must be clarified. These two concepts comprise the central theoretical problem in all military doctrine. Deterrence has been defined as the means of "discouraging the enemy from taking military action by posing for him a prospect of cost and risk outweighing his prospective gain."[4] Deterrence is essentially a psychological means of preventing war; it works more on the enemy's intentions than on how he plans his forces. The "deterrent value" of military forces is their ability to reduce the likelihood of enemy military moves. Defense has been defined as the means of "reducing our own prospective costs and risks in the event that deterrence fails."[5] Defense is the combative means of reducing the enemy's capability to inflict damage or deprivation. The "defense value" of military

forces is their ability to mitigate the adverse consequences of possible enemy moves, whether such consequences are counted as losses of territory or war damage.

Military doctrine is based on these two objectives: to deter enemy attacks and to defend, successfully, at minimum cost, against those attacks that occur. That different types of military force contribute in differing proportions to these two objectives often goes unnoticed in the formulation of military doctrine. As early as 1960, an American analyst pointed out that deterrence does not vary directly with the capacity for fighting war effectively and cheaply; a particular set of forces might produce strong deterrent effects and not provide a very effective "denial," the capacity to hold territory, or "damage-limiting" capability. Conversely, forces effective for defense might be less potent deterrents than other forces that might involve extremely high costs if used.[6] For example, to augment the deterrent value of nuclear weapons in Europe, it might be desirable to render automatic a response that the adversary recognizes as being costly for NATO, and communicate the fact of such automation to the adversary, thus reducing his doubts that we would actually choose to make this response when the occasion arose. Hence, a tactical nuclear response to conventional aggression in Europe might be made semiautomatic by thoroughly orienting NATO plans, organization, and strategy around this response, thereby increasing the difficulty of following a nonnuclear strategy in case of a Soviet challenge. But such automation would not be desirable for defense, which would require flexibility and freedom to choose the least costly action in the light of circumstances at the time of attack.[7]

How TNWs should meet the requirements of both deterrence and defense is the central theoretical problem of TNW military doctrine: In the event of an overwhelming Warsaw Pact conventional attack, can NATO employ its TNWs in defense of Western Europe such that the costs incurred are acceptable and limited? The selective use of nuclear weapons in Europe with the intention of confining the conflict to the tactical level is referred to as limited nuclear war. TNWs have traditionally been associated with limited, rather than general, nuclear war. General nuclear war is most commonly understood as a nuclear conflict between the superpowers involving direct attacks with strategic nuclear weapons on each other's homeland. Limited nuclear war refers to a nuclear conflict in which the homelands of the two superpowers will likely be inviolate. Applying this concept to NATO leaves Europe as the principal battleground for a limited nuclear war. Thus the underlying implication of TNWs designed to have a strong defense value is that NATO would be willing to incur the risks of a limited nuclear war.

Under NATO military doctrine of the 1950s, TNWs were considered a deterrent against a massive conventional attack by the Warsaw Pact. The first TNW, an atomic "cannon," was deployed in Europe in 1953. Because the Warsaw Pact has always maintained larger conventional forces than NATO, the Alliance saw no real prospect of matching these ground forces

with conventional weapons. The deterrent value of TNWs was based on increasing the enemy's cost expectation beyond what it would be if these forces were equipped only with conventional weapons. Although the purpose of TNWs was to offset Warsaw Pact superiority in conventional forces, their use was inextricably linked to employment of America's strategic nuclear arsenal. TNWs would serve as a trigger for an extension of U.S. strategic retaliatory forces to the European theater. The doctrine of massive retaliation presupposed that overwhelming nuclear superiority enabled the United States to fight and win a nuclear war against the Soviet Union and its allies. Since NATO assumed that the Soviet Union and the Warsaw Pact appreciated this proposition, nuclear weapons at that time needed only to have a strong deterrent value. Since conventional forces alone could not contain a Soviet attack, the deterrent value of TNWs was especially important to Western Europe's feeling of security. Given America's preponderance of strategic weaponry, the level of nuclear force appeared stable enough to prevent armed conflict in Europe.

By the late 1950s, however, the USSR was beginning to equip its ground forces with TNWs and was striving hard to establish a credible second-strike capability in the strategic realm. As the Soviets acquired the ability to resist total destruction of their nuclear arsenal in an initial nuclear attack, the previously unchallenged superiority of American strategic forces began to decline. With this perceived diminution of American nuclear power, the implications of a two-sided limited nuclear war in Europe emerged as a contentious issue in the Alliance.[8] The perception of a "missile gap" between the United States and the Soviet Union provided the context for heightened concern about the stability of the nuclear balance in Europe. Cause for concern about deterrence at levels of aggression below all-out strategic nuclear exchange was substantiated in two tactical nuclear war games conducted by NATO in 1955. The results strongly indicated that reliance on tactical nuclear defense would lead to devastation of the very Western Europe that NATO was designed to protect. The report of Operation Sage Brush concluded "that the destruction was so great that no such thing as limited or purely tactical nuclear war was possible in such an area."[9] European fears after the Carte Blanche war games stemmed from the conviction that the use of TNWs "will not defend Europe, but destroy it."[10] But an earlier conclusion from the theoretical studies of tactical nuclear warfare prevented American nuclear strategists from abandoning attempts to formulate a convincing rationale for their defense value. These studies had found that a conflict in which both sides possessed large numbers of TNWs would be far more destructive to Western Europe than a war distinguished by unilateral NATO use, primarily because the USSR had recently deployed TNWs with substantially greater yields and radiation effects.[11] Thus TNWs were deemed necessary not only to deter conventional attack but also to deter Soviet use of their new, more destructive TNWs.

Interest in TNWs was sustained by economic, political, and technological considerations even as their deterrent value began to wane.

The importance of budgetary considerations in the United States during the 1950s made the Eisenhower administration unwilling to contribute to the development of a non-nuclear deterrent sufficient to balance Soviet superiority in conventional forces. The reluctance of the United States to appropriate funds for an adequate conventional defense was exacerbated by the failure of the allies to meet the conventional force goals agreed upon at the Lisbon Conference in 1952. This attitude was in keeping with the "long-standing U.S. tradition of trading technology for manpower."[12] Breakthroughs in fusion technology in 1957 and completion of the design for an enhanced radiation warhead were evidence of the ongoing search for low-yield, discriminate weaponry that could provide better rationales for TNW employment. Progress in the development of "clean" weapons took two forms: attempts to reduce the materially destructive blast and heat effects of atomic explosives and efforts to limit civilian debilitation by radiation. Both are referred to as the limitation of collateral damage; however, until the late 1960s more emphasis was placed on eliminating excess destruction from heat and blast. Efforts to reduce residual radiation or fallout did not gain widespread support within the U.S. government until the early 1970s.

As the transatlantic debate on a suitable role for tactical nuclear weapons in Europe continued, of critical concern were the implications of a two-sided tactical nuclear war for conventional forces. Disagreement was rife as to whether the defense of Europe by TNWs required fewer or more conventional forces. While many European analysts continued to believe that conventional forces could easily be traded for tactical nuclear defense, a growing number of U.S. strategists held that a tactical nuclear war would dictate a much larger battlefield and generate substantially higher rates of attrition, thus necessitating more manpower, which neither the United States nor Europe were willing to provide. The increasingly doubtful validity of various rationales for the development and deployment of TNWs, along with a growing perception of strategic vulnerability during the "missile gap" period, prompted the Kennedy administration to put forward a new justification for these weapons.

This rationale, part of the concept of flexible response developed by Secretary of Defense Robert S. McNamara in the early 1960s, held that TNW served to enhance the credibility of the U.S. strategic deterrent by providing a link between the possible failure of conventional defense in Europe and U.S. willingness to employ its ultimate weapons. Under flexible response, conventional forces would be augmented to provide more reliable conventional defense, while the deterrent value of TNWs would be enhanced to assure Europe that the United States was committed to the preservation of NATO-Europe, should conventional defense fail. The doctrine held that a conflict with the Soviet Union should be confined to a conventional level if possible; thus McNamara embarked on a policy of conventional emphasis as the only

acceptable means of defense in the nuclear age. Conventional defense was for the first time established as the preferred riposte to aggression in Europe and elsewhere. Nuclear weapons, though still the option of last resort, were envisioned as insurance against the possible collapse of conventional defense rather than as NATO's first and only response to a major attack. Recall that the doctrine of massive retaliation presupposed the possibility of immediate employment of American nuclear forces in response to any form of major Soviet aggression. McNamara's concept of Mutual Assured Destruction (MAD) now became the sole criterion for designing U.S. strategic forces—the maintenance of a capability to destroy an enemy only after it had launched a full-scaled attack.

The role of TNWs during the Kennedy and Johnson administrations was to reinforce the credibility of the U.S. pledge to employ its strategic deterrent in defense of its European allies. Both administrations held that TNWs were "extremely destructive devices and hardly the preferred weapons to defend such heavily populated areas as Europe."[13] Moreover, they could not be meaningfully substituted for conventional forces. Both subscribed to the "firebreak" theory, which presumed that the wartime detonation of any nuclear device would lead to a strategic exchange; therefore, the real threshold in escalation lay not between the use of TNW and strategic weapons but rather between conventional and nuclear warfare. Thus early resort to TNWs was deemphasized. Conditions for use were restricted to situations in which "the opponent employs such weapons first, or any attack by conventional forces which put Europe in danger of being overrun."[14] The use of tactical nuclear weapons in the event of a collapse of conventional arms would constitute an intermediate and postnuclear threshold "link" to the strategic deterrent. The "linkage" value of TNW became an indispensable component of Alliance relations, assuaging European fears that the United States might not risk an attack on its homeland, through the use of it strategic forces, to defend Europe. This political role, however, overestimated their military utility as a viable instrument of defense.

Although McNamara enunciated the strategy of flexible response at the outset of the Kennedy administration, it was not formally adopted by NATO until 1967. The basic statement of current NATO military doctrine is embodied in this strategy. Military Committee document MC 14/3, "Overall Strategic Concept for the Defense of the NATO Area," adopted by the Defense Planning Committee in March 1967, commits NATO to:

- meet initially any aggression short of general nuclear attack with direct defense at a level—conventional or nuclear—chosen by the aggressor;
- conduct deliberate escalation if aggression cannot be contained and the situation restored by direct defense;
- initiate an appropriate general nuclear response to a major nuclear attack.

The debate over TNWs in the 1970s grew out of a dilemma inherent in this doctrine: Under what circumstances are TNWs to assume a defensive, as distinct from deterrent, role? More specifically, at what point during armed conflict with the Warsaw Pact would NATO be prepared to employ battlefield nuclear weapons? And how quickly would SACEUR (Supreme Allied Commander, Europe), who is always an American general, be prepared to escalate the conflict by employing longer-range weapons? The operational implications of the doctrine are, perhaps necessarily, vague. NATO and U.S. spokesmen have defended its ambiguity with regard to specific force postures on the grounds that it complicates Soviet planning with uncertainty. But perhaps a more plausible explanation for the ambiguity lies in the origins of flexible response.

First, flexible response is primarily a U.S.-inspired doctrine, the "McNamara" strategy. By the time of its formal adoption, NATO merely ratified existing unilateral U.S. force posture decisions. Second, flexible response was largely a U.S.-imposed doctrine. A time lag of six years existed between U.S. strategic revision in 1961 and NATO ratification in 1967. The intervening debate was so bitter that it contributed significantly to the military defection of France. The bitterness was reflected primarily in the acute European awareness of the reason for the U.S. initiative: the problem of emerging vulnerability of the United States to survivable Soviet strategic forces. Thus flexible response was designed in large part to deal with American strategic problems.

It was already clear by the late 1950s that the threat of massive retaliation was too blunt an instrument to deter limited provocations in Europe with any reliability. Improvements in Soviet delivery capabilities by the early 1960s meant that an American initiation of strategic nuclear war in response even to a serious attack in Western Europe risked an equally devastating Soviet riposte against the United States. Thus a deterrent posture relying primarily on U.S. strategic nuclear power became increasingly incredible. The extension of McNamara's idea of suitable responses at various possible levels of confrontation in Europe contained the implication that the United States wanted to reduce the allies' reliance on the American strategic nuclear umbrella. As European concern mounted over the credibility of the U.S. strategic deterrent, insurmountable fears of "decoupling" suggested that the United States might not invoke its strategic arsenal against a Soviet attack that could not be contained by NATO's conventional forces. Many Europeans viewed this revision of NATO doctrine as an attempt to hedge American risks.

Of great significance is the fact that adoption of flexible response was achieved by framing the doctrine in terms ambiguous enough to enable various interpretations and thus accomodate different interests. Ambiguity was the greatest in the role of TNWs. Both the United States and Europe agreed on its importance, but for opposite reasons: For the United States, TNWs offered the

hope of limiting a land war short of strategic catastrophe; in the European point of view, TNWs represented the best assurance that a European war would threaten the USSR with general nuclear war by escalation. MC 14/3 and subsequent NATO nuclear guidelines could accommodate either view; however, the inherent contradictions effectively foreclosed attempts to derive from declaratory policy precise guidance concerning the way in which TNWs might ultimately be employed.

At the heart of this ambiguity, and the debate over flexible response, lay a fundamental disagreement between the United States and the allies regarding the nature of deterrence and how its risks should be apportioned. At issue were two polar approaches to the problem of deterrence. The first, manifested in its pure form by massive retaliation, grounded deterrence in the threat of punishment, that is, the willingness of the United States to apply its nuclear power directly against the Soviet homeland. The second approach, implicit in the American interpretation of flexible response, sought deterrence by the denial of objectives. It implied maintaining a conventional capability adequate to deny Soviet arms physical access to NATO territory or to make penetration intolerably expensive to the Soviet Union. The implicit consequence of this approach, should deterrence fail, is a war fought on European territory, rather than between two superpowers.

From the point of view of American strategists, deterrence-by-threat-of-punishment had two drawbacks. Since flexible response posed the threat of a possible, but not definite, maximum-risk response to any provocation, it risked being incapable of deterring anything less than outright, massive aggression. Yet if the Soviets nevertheless believed the escalatory threat, the posture implied enormous instability in a local crisis, because the aggressor would have an incentive to preempt an anticipated NATO nuclear initiation. In such an event, the United States might unintentionally provoke nuclear war over a relatively minor confrontation. These drawbacks seemed to point to the need for a substantial capability to contain the aggressor without resort to general nuclear response. But deterrence-by-denial posed equally severe drawbacks from the European perspective. It threatened to undermine deterrence by reducing the aggressor's risks; the existence of a substantial conventional capability would lessen the credibility of American willingness to engage its strategic nuclear forces in the defense of Europe. Moreover, deterrence-by-denial translated into a land war on NATO territory, promising to make Western Europe the battlefield once again, while the superpowers remained relatively unscathed.

The theoretical distinction between competing deterrence postures was not easily maintained in practice, especially given the possession by both sides of a wide diversity of theater nuclear capabilities. The intra-alliance debate tried to resolve issues of flexible response by making a virtue of ambiguity. By asserting the continuity of the conflict spectrum and grounding deterrence in the risk

that any confrontation, however small, might—but need not—escalate to general nuclear war, flexible response satisfied both European insistence on the centrality of the strategic nuclear deterrent and the American desire to hedge the risk of its use.

The susceptibility of flexible response to widely divergent interpretations posed a number of practical problems for NATO. For one, the Alliance was unable to define precisely the guidelines for employing TNWs. Understandably, Europeans desired a voice in the use of nuclear weapons on their territory. Transatlantic debates over the control of TNWs culminated in a formal agreement in 1969 on general guidelines for consultation procedures on the use of nuclear weapons in Europe. The decision process controlling the release of NATO's nuclear weapons has been and continues to be a source of contention among the allies. Except for a small British force, NATO's nuclear weapons are controlled by the United States. The authority to employ these weapons is vested in SACEUR, upon direction from the president of the United States and consultation with the allies. SACEUR is simultaneously the commander of NATO and of U.S. forces in Europe. He is also the allied commander responsible to NATO's Defense Planning Committee, the allied forum for consultation on the use of nuclear force in Europe. The ability of SACEUR to order the release of nuclear weapons has always been slightly ambiguous due to the nature of the constraints on his dual role. While the allies can make recommendations, the release of nuclear weapons must be sanctioned by the U.S. president. Irreconcilable controversies over authority for nuclear release were a major reason for the French withdrawal from NATO's integrated military command in 1966. U.S. officials have long feared that allied leaders would veto SACEUR's request for nuclear release authority during a crisis or would delay their response so long that NATO would be unable to disperse its nuclear weapons to less vulnerable locations prior to aggression. Europeans, on the other hand, have been concerned either that the American president would not respond quickly enough to an allied request for their use or that, in a crisis situation, the United States would attempt to order their use without prior consultation.

Another practical problem essential to the role of TNWs was explaining the purposes of NATO's conventional force posture. Of critical importance was the point at which NATO might escalate the land battle from conventional to nuclear weapons, commonly known as the nuclear threshold. This issue was never resolved under flexible response. Europeans interpreted MC 14/3 as calling for conventional defense only against a limited Warsaw Pact attack. In the event of a massive invasion, they envisaged a rapid escalation to general nuclear war. This interpretation was consistent with the European preference for deterrence-by-threat-of-punishment and served the additional purpose of foreclosing the necessity to maintain substantial conventional ground forces. In contrast, the United States interpreted flexible

response as requiring the maintenance of a conventional capability, and, since the Nixon administration, of a short-range nuclear capability, adequate to contain even a massive Warsaw Pact attack for a substantial period. But even the U.S. military establishment was uncomfortable with this requirement. The result was serious asymmetries in areas such as ammunition stocks and command and control of TNWs.

A third difficulty with flexible response lay in the definition of forward defense, to which all NATO members were nominally committed. Forward defense suggests that NATO will defend allied territory by holding a line as close to the German border as possible. For West Germany, forward defense means defense at the frontier, as far from population centers as possible. Germany's shallow geographic depth, lack of natural barriers, urbanized demography, and proximity of major industrial areas to the border make anything less politically intolerable. Since few European planners believed that NATO would be able to conduct a successful conventional defense against a serious Soviet thrust, they argued for the declaratory willingness to escalate rapidly across the nuclear threshold. Yet NATO plans have always included the option of counterattacking with TNWs without specifying when the conflict would be escalated to the strategic level, if a Warsaw Pact attack were to succeed in forcing NATO armies back, and conventional forces could not halt an assault: "NATO must be capable of executing an effective nuclear attack against Warsaw Pact military forces with discrimination and limited collateral damage, in response to a major conventional attack or limited nuclear attack."[15] Thus how far "forward" forward defense needs to be in order to defend with conventional forces against a Warsaw Pact incursion has been a point of contention between the United States and its allies. To effectively deter by threatening a limited nuclear response to conventional attack might not require the stationing of conventional forces at the border. This disagreement over forward defense produced a variety of force posture inconsistencies. With respect to TNWs, these inconsistencies became unmanageable in the ERW debate. For example, both proponents and opponents of ERWs in West Germany used the "escalation" argument to substantiate their positions on these weapons; the former contended that ERWs would strengthen the chain of escalation from conventional to tactical to strategic nuclear weapons. Opponents of the weapon argued that the United States would interpret their employment doctrine more loosely in order not to invoke its strategic nuclear forces once TNWs had been used.

Thus the apparent doctrinal consensus on flexible response was beset by real disagreement from the beginning. Thereafter, developments in the strategic environment only exacerbated the problem. Vietnam had a major impact on Alliance strategy as well. American involvement in Vietnam cut deeply into the American commitment to NATO, reducing U.S. divisions deployed to or earmarked for NATO from 14 to 9. In addition, resources

available in Europe to support training and maintenance evaporated as combat in Vietnam intensified. Since Soviet conventional strength in Europe increased markedly during the same period, the effect was to undermine the American argument for greater NATO reliance on conventional forces.[16]

NATO's recognition of Soviet nuclear parity in the late 1960s had tremendous psychological implications for all Alliance members. Parity intensified the U.S. desire to avoid strategic nuclear exchange and aggravated Europe's sensitivity to American action that appeared to do so at their expense. Parity thus reinforced both sides in their already divergent interpretations of the common doctrine and rendered still more perilous efforts to reconcile them.

In the face of these difficulties, the theater nuclear capability appeared to hold Alliance strategy together. By the late 1960s the United States had deployed 7,000 nuclear weapons in Europe, ranging in yield from less than 1 kiloton to well over 100 and capable of delivery by cannon, missile, and aircraft, or of emplacement as giant land mines. These weapons allowed NATO to maintain the fiction of a flexible response capability despite manifest conventional weaknesses. That the theater nuclear posture was supported by no viable employment doctrine, that the conventional forces it presumably supported were neither trained nor equipped to operate in an intense nuclear environment, and that the use of these weapons and their Soviet counterparts would almost certainly leave much of NATO territory in ruins was well known by both American and European planners. Yet the facts were ignored by general consensus: Europe refusing to entertain the notion of a purely local nuclear conflict and the United States fearing that attempts to redress deficiencies in TNWs would demolish arguments for a strong conventional option.

In sum, by the time President Nixon assumed office, the gap between NATO's declaratory strategy and the military capabilities that presumably gave it effect had grown dangerously wide. The risk that the fragile doctrinal consensus might rupture altogether loomed very large on both sides of the Atlantic. The Alliance debate of the 1970s over the purpose of TNWs under flexible response coincided with an American debate over the function of strategic nuclear weapons and of conventional forces. The doctrinal significance of ERWs grew out of these related debates.

The Nixon administration entered office with a public mandate to extricate the United States from Vietnam and a strong preelection commitment to revitalize the Atlantic Alliance. Although these objectives would, at first glance, appear to be highly compatible—ending the war would free attention and resources for reallocation to NATO—the problem was much more complicated. Vietnam had long-term consequences as well as direct effects on the Alliance. They included a general American dissatisfaction with the scale of U.S. overseas commitments; a growing domestic crisis posing the need for revision of national spending priorities; mounting pressure from an overextended economy, manifested by increasing

inflation and large trade and monetary deficits; and finally, deep weariness with the military in general, fed by the apparent inability of America's massive military power to produce foreign policy successes. By 1969 some of the implications of these diffuse trends for American defense policy were already evident: mounting opposition to defense spending, strong political pressure to end conscription, and increasing congressional support for U.S. troop reduction, most immediately related to NATO. Together these developments implied that even a swift conclusion of the Vietnam War would not automatically remedy NATO's malaise.

Two salient conclusions emerged from an examination of America's worldwide defense posture by the revitalized National Security Council in 1969. With regard to the strategic balance, American recapture of strategic nuclear superiority in any meaningful sense was not a feasible objective, politically and economically. Thus the administration decided to accept the concept of strategic "sufficiency," in effect ratifying the parity condition, and to seek negotiated arms limitation at the earliest possible opportunity. The second assessment concerned the role of general-purpose forces, central to the flexible response concept for NATO. Conventional forces had to be reduced, owing primarily to the staggering upward pressure on the defense budget. The bulk of the cut was made in high-cost, labor-intensive conventional forces, especially the Army, certainly not favorably received by allied governments.

The dilemma over how to apportion these cuts led to a contraction of regional responsibilities to which U.S. conventional forces were committed. In 1970, after the United States reassigned priority to the European, rather than Asian, theater, the administration embarked on a major effort to revitalize the NATO deterrent. This effort had three components: to refurbish the conventional posture by emphasizing qualitative improvements in conventional weapons, to find a way to restore a deterrent value to the American strategic nuclear umbrella, and to modernize the tactical nuclear stockpile.

The immediate requirement was to halt the erosion of NATO's conventional posture. The administration had to refute the claim of both U.S. and European planners that NATO was incapable of defending conventionally against a Warsaw Pact attack. From this belief flowed another: that such an attack must quickly lead to nuclear war. To refute this claim, the administration attempted to redefine NATO's threat analysis by arguing that the threat from the Warsaw Pact was overstated. For example, American spokesmen contended that massive Soviet advantages in tanks were partially offset by greater NATO antitank capabilities, soon to be boosted by enhanced radiation warheads, an antitank weapon. Since the Warsaw Pact's conventional improvements were largely technological—new armored vehicles and artillery, new fighters and bombers—the administration argued that NATO's conventional deficiency was largely qualitative and that specific improvements would help resolve the problem, provided existing manpower levels were maintained.

Although the allies in general accepted the program of conventional force improvement, they were nonetheless concerned that a renewed emphasis on conventional forces implied nuclear decoupling, especially in light of SALT I. The administration then turned to the other component of NATO's defense posture: reestablishment of the extended strategic deterrent. Secretary of Defense James Schlesinger argued that even though vulnerable to nuclear retaliation, the United States could use its strategic forces to deter Soviet aggression, provided Washington could demonstrate the willingness and capability to use these forces selectively. By threatening to employ nuclear weapons discriminately and at a carefully regulated pace, the United States could raise the costs of aggression beyond any benefit Soviet decision makers might hope to gain. The principle of deterrence in this modification of nuclear strategy was uncertainty: The adversary would never be able completely to uncover American intentions. Thus as long as the United States retained its ultimate capacity to destroy Soviet society in total, Soviet decision makers would have an incentive to restrain their own use of strategic nuclear weapons. Out of the reformulation of strategic doctrine, known as "Limited Nuclear Options," emerged the proposition that NATO should be able to convince its adversaries that if a massive conventional invasion in Europe forced NATO to use nuclear weapons, the ensuing conflict could be controlled without causing unacceptable levels of damage to West Europe. The idea was to increase the number of available options for deterrence and defense, thereby increasing the uncertainty in the adversary's calculus of Western intentions.

Prompted by changes in the strategic environment, new conventional and nuclear weapons technologies, and by Schlesinger's clearly stated expression of dissatisfaction with the current tactical nuclear posture in and for NATO-Europe (with urgency added by the terms of the Nunn Admendment),[17] the United States then embarked on a TNW modernization program. The guiding principles of this program were outlined in Schlesinger's April 1975 report to Congress, *The Theater Nuclear Force Posture in Europe*. The purpose of TNWs was explicitly defined in terms of both deterrence and defense: "Theater nuclear forces deter and defend against theater nuclear attacks; help deter and, if necessary, defend against conventional attack; and help deter conflict escalation."[18] The type of deterrence prescribed by Schlesinger was that which Europe regarded with fearful contempt, deterrence-by-denial:

> We would prefer to deter through provision of direct defense and denial of Warsaw Pact military gains (e.g., seizure of territory), rather than deterrence only through the threat of escalation and all-out retaliatory attacks on Warsaw Pact resources—though these latter options will be maintained.[19]

In other sections of the report Schlesinger emphasized the strength of the American commitment to NATO-Europe, in order to allay possible fears that

the United States intended to make deterrence-by-denial the only guiding principle of TNWs in Europe: "U.S. nuclear weapons in Europe are a visible symbol to Allies and adversaries of the U.S. commitment to provide for Europe's nuclear defense."[20] Under what circumstances this nuclear defense would be confined to the European battlefield or escalated to the strategic level was, as in MC 14/3, left unspecified.

Discussion in NATO from the time of this report until the ERW became a public issue generally avoided the still unresolved doctrinal dilemmas largely because neither side wanted to upset the fragile consensus that existed only on the actual existence of TNWs in Europe, not on their purposes. As one analyst noted, "unambiguous and rigorously argued TNW doctrines have an uncomfortable tendency to state bluntly what NATO members would really prefer to leave shrouded in discreet silence, if not mystery."[21] This attitude allowed the increasing divergence of U.S. and European interests in TNWs to go unattended. To many American defense officials, planning for the selective employment of TNWs against a range of hypothetical military and political situations seemed eminently reasonable and necessary. Such plans would potentially permit the controlled use of nuclear weapons at low levels of violence without necessarily entailing widespread destruction and escalation to general nuclear war. For obvious reasons, Europeans do not wish to be defended by extensive TNW use. Rather, they see TNWs providing a credible link between the NATO forces deployed in Europe and the strategic forces of the United States. This posture would preclude the need to provide seriously for the physical defense of Western Europe. So NATO strategy has tried to accomodate the tensions between these two sets of vital interests by allowing for various interpretations.

This doctrinal shift, placing more emphasis on nuclear weapons as an instrument of defense, did, however, receive some criticism in the United States, though much of it focused on the Limited Nuclear Options Strategy as it applied to strategic nuclear weapons. Critics took issue with the possibility of fighting a limited nuclear war implied by the doctrinal shift, and their arguments were germane to tactical, as well as strategic, nuclear weapons. The most persuasive criticism attacked a fundamental premise of what is known as a "nuclear emphasis defense" and was crucial to the employment policy for TNWs: that nuclear war, once begun, could be controlled by an act of will. Skeptics pointed out that such a claim imputed substantial self-restraint to Soviet decision makers and ignored the mentally destabilizing effects of fear, anger, and uncertainty that nuclear attack, however limited, might produce.[22] Those who supported a "nuclear emphasis defense" did not necessarily argue that nuclear war could be controlled, but rather that TNWs must attempt to serve this purpose:

> . . . the essential question . . . has to do with . . . whether or not tactical nuclear war is a feasible option. There are some people who think once it goes

nuclear, it is going to go strategic and there is no in-between thing. There are other people who think it would be better to have some in-between option.[23]

Whether the limited use of nuclear weapons can be both effective against a massive conventional attack and confined to the substrategic level is the crux of the allied controversy over the rationales for TNWs.

Another major issue was the credibility of the new defense-oriented TNWs as deterrents. The principal feature giving these weapons a greater defense value was their ability to restrict collateral damage and thereby reduce the likelihood of escalation. Proponents of these weapons maintained that by reducing the intended damage to civilian facilities, the weapons' deterrent value would be improved because the Warsaw Pact (WP) would have more reason to believe that NATO would in fact use its nuclear capability. The assumption is that the collateral damage caused by the limited and discriminate use of TNWs is less than the destruction of a widespread conventional conflict. The greater the credibility of a tactical nuclear defense, Schlesinger argued in 1975, the greater its deterrent value and the lower the likelihood of war:

> Since the tactical use of nuclear weapons may involve detonation on NATO territory, reduction of collateral damage should make it more credible to the WP that the Alliance will use nuclear weapons. Further, if deterrence fails, weapons with low collateral damage would reduce civilian casualities and perhaps reduce the risks of uncontrolled escalation. . . .
>
> Further reductions in collateral damage can be made by improvements in weapons systems (e.g., reduced yields, special warhead effects such as *enhanced radiation*, improved delivery system accuracy). However, it is necessary to keep in mind that NATO attempts to reduce collateral damage might not be matched by corresponding changes in WP capabilities or targeting doctrine.[24] [Emphasis added.]

The easily overlooked qualification in the last sentence points to the recognition that reduction of collateral damage might be meaningless for defense since the Warsaw Pact would still rely on its higher–yield, more destructive TNWs in any two-sided limited nuclear conflict. Critics contended that NATO's use of TNWs in a limited context might not save NATO forces from defeat by an overwhelming conventional attack without provoking devastating Soviet nuclear retaliation. They also claimed that by reducing collateral damage and enhancing the credibility of TNWs, the likelihood of their actually being used is greater. Their value as a deterrent depends on decreasing NATO's alleged reluctance to use nuclear weapons in the event of conventional failure. To the extent that NATO would be less reluctant to authorize the release of ERWs than of other TNWs (which is highly doubtful), these weapons lower the nuclear threshold. Critics charged that tampering with the distinction between conventional and nuclear warfare is dangerous;

the nuclear threshold should be clearly demarcated and maintained sufficiently high to forestall all but "last resort" rationales for crossing it. The weapons' supporters rebutted that making a nuclear option more viable reduced the likelihood of any war at all, and thus raised the nuclear threshold.

These ambiguities surrounding TNW employment helped to resurrect the entire debate on the role of nuclear weapons in Europe in the mid-70s. NATO had still not come to grips with its central doctrinal issue: how far NATO should be prepared to rely on nonnuclear forces to deter, and if necessary, defend against aggression from the East. The principal doctrinal dilemma facing the Alliance on battlefield nuclear weaponry such as the ERW was whether the perceived gains for deterrence associated with these weapons outweighed the perceived risks of a lowered nuclear threshold. Although the United States was in the midst of a TNW modernization program in the mid-1970s, these issues had not been resolved. Direct discussion of the concepts underlying this program was avoided in the Alliance because its implications would disrupt efforts to appear politically unified. Successive U.S. administrations had evaded rather than resolved the ambiguity at the heart of flexible response. Instead, while consistently asserting NATO's conventional defensibility, the Nixon administration advanced both a strategic and tactical nuclear doctrine whose only logical presumption was conventional failure. It simultaneously proposed to modernize its deployed theater nuclear stockpile, whose military value was obscure, diverting attention from conventional force improvement efforts, lowering the nuclear threshold, and still further undermining the credibility of its own alleged confidence in NATO's nonnuclear capability. The increasing difficulties in defining the rationales that should govern TNW deployment prompted such cynical comments as: "If they [TNWs] did not exist, it is far from certain that NATO would, today, seek to develop and deploy them."[25] This was the legacy that President Carter inherited in 1977.

NOTES

1. *Fiscal Year 1974 Authorization*, Hearings before the Senate Committee on Armed Services, 93rd Cong., 1st sess., 1973, pt. 2, p. 566.

2. Washington *Star*, July 8, 1977, cited in U.S. Congress, Senate, Senator Mark O. Hatfield speaking for the Amendment of the Public Works Appropriation 1978, 95th Cong., 1st sess., *Congressional Record*, July 13, 1977, S11742.

3. U.S. Congress, Senate, Committee on Armed Services, *Department of Defense Authorization for Appropriations for Fiscal Year 1979*, 95th Cong., 1st sess., 1978, p. 6545.

4. Glenn H. Snyder, *Deterrence and Defense: Toward a Theory of National Security* (Princeton, N.J.: Princeton University Press, 1961), p. 3.

5. Ibid.

6. Ibid, p. 4.

7. Ibid, p. 7.

8. Although the first theoretical studies of a limited nuclear war on the battlefield had been conducted in 1948, the principal concern at that time was the deterrence of large-scale aggression in Europe.

9. P. M. S. Blackett, *Studies of War* (London: Oliver and Boyd, 1962), p. 63.

10. Helmut Schmidt, *Defense or Retaliation: A German View* (New York: Praeger, 1962), p. 101.

11. Jeffrey Record, *U.S. Nuclear Weapons in Europe: Issues and Alternatives* (Washington, D. C.: The Brookings Institution, 1974), p. 10.

12. Ibid, p. 9.

13. Testimony of Secretary of Defense McNamara, *DoD Appropriations for 1964*, Hearing before the Subcommittee of the Committee on Appropriations, 88th Cong., 1st sess., 1963, p. 102.

14. Ibid.

15. Annual Department of Defense Report, Fiscal Year 1977, p. 103.

16. Richard Hart Sinnreich, "NATO's Evolving Nuclear Strategy," in *Nuclear Strategy and National Security: Points of View*, ed. Robert J. Pranger and Roger P. Labrie (Washington, D. C.: American Enterprise Institute for Public Policy Research, 1977), p. 308.

17. The Nunn Amendment to the Military Authorization Bill for Fiscal Year 1975, PL93-365, August 5, 1974, required, *inter alia*, that the secretary of defense "study the overall concept for use of TNWs in Europe," and "how the use of such weapons relates to deterrence and to a strong conventional defense."

18. James R. Schlesinger, *The Theater Nuclear Force Posture in Europe. A Report to the U.S. Congress*, April 1975, quoted in Pranger and Labrie, p. 168.

19. Ibid, p. 176.

20. Ibid, p. 185.

21. Colin S. Gray, "Theater Nuclear Weapons: Doctrines and Postures," *World Politics* 28 (January 1976): 301.

22. Sinnreich, p. 316.

23. Major General Frank A. Camm, *Military Applications of Nuclear Technology*, Hearings before the Subcommittee on Military Applications of the Joint Committee on Atomic Energy, 93rd Cong., 1st sess., April 16, 1973, pt. 1, p. 13.

24. Schlesinger, p. 184.

25. Gray, p. 301.

2

The Acquisition of
Enhanced Radiation Warheads:
Constraints and Incentives

A review of the military applications of enhanced radiation technology since its inception in 1958 reveals that technological concepts for constructing weapons suitable for tactical nuclear use were available long before the U.S. government began seriously to plan for the selective use of TNWs. The adaptation of technology to specific weapons systems and the formulation of military doctrine is a symbiotic process. Military doctrine is a combination of both the theoretical and the practical: On the one hand, there is the abstract distinction between deterrence and defense and a seemingly "rational" calculus of the structure of costs and benefits needed to deter and defend against a potential attacker. On the other hand, technological advances are continuously enlarging the scope of military capabilities, often subtly transforming the practical application of military doctrine. The acquisition of weapons with enhanced radiation features as part of the TNW modernization program of the 1970s was caused as much by organizational and political support for the technology itself as by the existence of a suitable doctrine defining the weapon's political and military utility.

Modernization of nuclear weapons is an evolutionary process. As technological concepts are perfected, they are adapted to new or existing weaponry. The development of the enhanced radiation concept was part of a broad trend in tactical nuclear weaponry toward the elimination of large-scale destruction from the use of nuclear weapons. Seen in the context of this general movement toward so-called clean nuclear weaponry, ERWs were just another outgrowth of this technological evolution. Numerous attempts since the late 1950s to incorporate enhanced radiation technology into viable weapons

systems had failed, owing to controversy over its military utility and to a lack of interest by politicians and high-level civilian defense officials. By the mid-1970s, however, the TNW modernization program provided the momentum for the fruition of earlier efforts by the scientific and military communities to apply the enhanced radiation concept to a viable weapons system. The technology was ready and available and U.S. nuclear strategy seemed finally to be moving in a direction in which the tactical use of nuclear weapons would be acceptable. The scientists, armed service representatives, and civilian defense officials who lobbied for the weapon couched their arguments in purely technical, military terms; they were not responsible for conducting analyses of the political implications of new weaponry. What concerned them was the application of enhanced radiation technology to battlefield weaponry. But as a weapon designed for tactical nuclear defense, ERWs came to symbolize the general dilemma surrounding TNWs in Alliance strategy, the dilemma that revolved around the central question of deterrence and defense: Can and should NATO prepare to engage in a limited nuclear war?

Enhanced radiation technology was not an innovation of the 1970s. Samuel T. Cohen, who participated in the Manhattan Project at the Los Alamos Laboratory, and has come to be known as the "Father of the neutron bomb," performed the study that, in 1958, led to the formulation of the concept of enhanced radiation. The term "neutron bomb" was apparently coined by the scientific community when the enhanced radiation concept was in its early stages of development. The term first appeared in the press in May 1959 when US News & World Report reported on the "neutron 'death ray' bomb which would kill man with streams of poisonous radiation, while leaving machines and buildings undamaged."[1] The neutron principle channels a greater portion of the energy of a nuclear explosion away from blast, heat, and radioactive fallout toward instant, high-energy radiation. The release of large quantities of energy by a nuclear explosion is produced by one of two processes: fission or fusion. Fission involves the splitting of atomic nuclei whereas fusion is the union of atomic nuclei to form heavier particles. The atom bomb is a fission device; the hydrogen, or thermonuclear, bomb is a fusion device. All nuclear explosives release destructive energy in four forms: blast, thermal radiation (heat), residual nuclear radiation (fallout and other contaminated materials), and initial nuclear radiation. The original nuclear explosives used in Japan were standard fission devices, in which the distribution of the four effects is approximately 50 percent blast, 35 percent heat, 10 percent residual nuclear radiation, and 5 percent initial nuclear radiation. The enhanced radiation concept evolved from efforts to tailor the energy of a fusion explosion so that, instead of heat and blast, its primary product is a burst of neutrons in the form of initial nuclear radiation. The enhanced radiation warhead is designed to maintain the same radius of destruction as much larger standard fission devices, but with proportionately reduced blast, heat, and residual radiation

effects. The distribution of the four effects in a *pure* fusion explosion (one that requires no fissile material) would be approximately 20 percent blast and 80 percent initial nuclear radiation. The battlefield ERWs developed in the 1970s require a small fission "trigger" to set off the fusion reaction. The energy released by this weapon is approximately 40 percent blast, 25 percent thermal radiation, 30 percent initial nuclear radiation, and 5 percent fallout.[2]

The incentive in the late 1950s for the development of low-yield TNWs, utilizing both fission and fusion reactions, was the realization that the first fission TNWs deployed in Europe in 1953 had yields so high that the destruction they would cause in a European conflict would be greater than any reasonable objectives. This conclusion was confirmed in the 1955 NATO war game "Carte Blanche," in which immediate West German casualties from the detonation of 268 weapons were estimated at 1.5 million dead and 3.5 million wounded.[3] A movement composed mainly of U.S. scientists and growing to include members of the civilian defense community and NATO military planners sought to explore ways of limiting collateral damage and maintaining the desired amount of destructive potential. The enhanced radiation concept was part of this broader trend toward low-yield weaponry, utilizing both fission and fusion devices. The objective was the perfection of weaponry that could be used at the front line against enemy troops in a far more discriminating manner than larger tactical nuclear weapons of the standard fission type.

From its inception, however, the neutron bomb concept had been a political football, being tossed around within the three armed services (Air Force, Army, and Navy) and being used by Congress to oppose the Eisenhower administration's support for a nuclear test ban. The neutron bomb concept was valued in both these battles—interservice rivalry and executive-legislative feuding—not so much for its potential military capabilities but as an instrument for furthering another cause. Throughout the 1950s the principal nuclear mission for US forces was controlled by the Air Force, which, dominated by the Strategic Air Command (SAC) and its fleet of strategic bombers, saw no value in low-yield tactical nuclear weaponry that would not enhance SAC's mission of being able to inflict massive retaliation upon the Soviet Union. In the early 1950s, the Army had begun to acquire a large stockpile of relatively high-yield nondiscriminate tactical nuclear weapons for U.S. forces in Europe and had thus already made significant progress toward defining its nuclear role. Only the Navy, having been forced out of strategic bombing by SAC, was still in search of a nuclear mission and was simultaneously groping for a way to justify the role of the aircraft carrier. Thus the Navy rapidly embraced the enhanced radiation concept as a means of proving that its carrier-based aircraft could provide a credible and effective tactical nuclear capability.[4] It was a Navy captain who became Sam Cohen's sponsor during these early years of trying to sell the neutron bomb concept to the Eisenhower administration.

Since the discovery of the enhanced radiation concept, the scientific community, in particular Sam Cohen, had been searching for suitable military

applications of this new technology. Such efforts were actively pursued by the Lawrence Livermore Laboratory in two projects, code-named "Dove" and "Starling." In 1959 the Los Alamos and Lawrence Livermore Laboratories, under the direction of the Atomic Energy Commission (AEC), urged the Department of Defense to establish requirements for the research and development of neutron warheads. The spokesman for the laboratories, Edward Teller, promised President Eisenhower that if approval of the test ban treaty was delayed, then the nuclear weapons labs would be able to develop "clean" tactical nuclear weapons within a relatively short period. A former member of Eisenhower's Science Advisory Committee recalls that the majority of the group was not interested in Teller's offer.[5] This lack of interest likely was the result of Eisenhower's determination to reach a test ban treaty with the Soviet Union.

Promotion of the neutron bomb concept, however, continued to be the focal point of efforts by the AEC, the Joint Chiefs of Staff (JCS), and the Joint Committee on Atomic Energy (JCAE) to end the moratorium on nuclear weapons testing that Eisenhower had mandated in 1958. On July 19, 1959, in the first accurate media coverage of the development of the neutron bomb, the Washington Post summarized the political context in which the neutron bomb had already gained its notoriety:

> If such a weapon is possible, as it now appears to be, it may make attempt to set up a total nuclear test ban as a first step toward disarmament meaningless, since tests on large weapons of this type could be concealed underground. And the low-blast effect would make them difficult to detect. . . . The need for further tests to perfect this type of bomb may have been responsible for some of the opposition to a total nuclear test ban now being discussed by the three nuclear powers, the United States, Great Britain and the Soviet Union, at Geneva. . . .[6]

Support for the neutron bomb continued to grow into the early 1960s as various factions in Congress and the Pentagon sought to defeat efforts by the Eisenhower and Kennedy administrations to conclude a test ban treaty. In the fall of 1960, Thomas Murray, a former AEC commissioner, wrote an open letter to presidential candidates Nixon and Kennedy advocating development of the neutron bomb and termination of the nuclear test moratorium. "Conceptual designs for this new type of [neutron] weapon have existed in American laboratories. They would have already been tested, had it not been for our test moratorium. The moratorium has effectively blocked American advance to a new position of military and political strength."[7] Senator Thomas Dodd, who led the congressional campaign against the test ban treaty, wrote several letters to President Kennedy urging him to consider the potential "revolutionary military impact" of the neutron bomb and thus to reconsider

his support for the test ban treaty.[8] Dodd claimed that "on the single issue of the neutron bomb might hang the survival of the Free World."[9] By 1961 efforts by the defense community to defeat the test moratorium had increased to a level where even the Air Force was willing to actively endorse the neutron bomb. Proponents of neutron bomb development received a temporary boost to their efforts when the Soviet Union ended the nuclear test moratorium on September 1, 1961. In 1962 the Lawrence Livermore Laboratory conducted the first underground tests of a neutron device in Nevada.

By spring of 1963 the lab was ready to test a device that could be "weaponized" for use with such battlefield delivery systems as a bomb dropped from tactical aircraft and surface-to-surface missiles like the Honest John and Lance, the latter still under development. This early neutron device was apparently not applicable to the artillery projectiles for which it would be designed in the 1970s.[10] The next step in the development process was to find a customer for the neutron bomb. Following successful testing, the director of the Lawrence Livermore Laboratory requested that AEC Chairman Glenn Seaborg ask the Pentagon to evaluate the neutron bomb for incorporation into a suitable delivery system.[11] This request led to a JCS study that recommended that the Defense Department establish requirements for the neutron warhead. But another study, conducted by the Office of Systems Analysis, headed by Alain Enthoven, a close advisor to Secretary McNamara, did not reach such favorable conclusions on the development of the neutron bomb. Sam Cohen has suggested that the conclusions of the Enthoven study were due in large part to Enthoven's close relationship with McNamara, who sought to reduce NATO's reliance on tactical nuclear weapons.[12] Moreover, an Army colonel was put in charge of the study and, at that time, support for the neutron bomb could have jeopardized the Army's attempts to get a higher-yield fission warhead approved for its new Lance missile.[13] The JCS did not contest the Enthoven study, whose conclusions were allowed to stand.

Meanwhile, congressional opponents of the test ban treaty were still lobbying vigorously for the neutron bomb. Senator Dodd urged the Kennedy Administration to match the Soviets in enhanced radiation technology, because they had apparently "embarked upon such a development more than a decade ago."[14] The consequences of facing an adversary who possessed such weapons without a similar capability were alleged to be "either to retreat precipitously or to strike back with our much more limited number of heavier nuclear weapons and destroy the whole country."[15] The United States had thus far limited development of low-yield TNWs because they were not cost effective; it was "cheaper to make a big bang than a small one"[16] under the fission process. Proponents of low-yield TNW development, such as Senator Thomas Dodd, responded that the United States "must face up to the harsh realities of the nuclear age by striving to maintain our nuclear superiority."[17]

Dodd's arguments in support of the neutron bomb foreshadow those that were made in later public debates. His fundamental premise was the need to be able to fight a limited nuclear war, taking advantage of technological developments in low-yield, discriminate weaponry. These innovations, he contended, would enable NATO to use small tactical nuclear weapons like the neutron bomb without escalation to strategic exchange.[18] He listed four advantages of the neutron bomb over the then-deployed TNWs that would give it "revolutionary implications": reduced cost of tactical fusion weapons; greater military effectiveness; less damage to the allies' urban centers; and relatively insignificant fallout.[19] He cited a 1958 report by a Soviet physicist, indicating that research on fission-free nuclear explosives in the USSR dated back to 1952. The United States, Dodd claimed, had no choice but to develop the neutron bomb because "the nation that does not have it will be faced with a choice between surrender or starting an all-out nuclear war."[20]

The American rationale for nuclear weapons in Europe has always been a source of anxiety for the Europeans. According to Dodd, NATO's need for the neutron bomb in 1963 was the result of an inadequate conventional defense and the declining credibility of the American strategic nuclear umbrella. Although the United States was, at that time, in the midst of restructuring and improving NATO's conventional defenses, Dodd claimed that: "our NATO allies simply do not have confidence in their ability to match the Communist bloc in military manpower or conventional capabilities."[21] Moreover, European confidence in the American strategic nuclear deterrent was waning as a result of the Kennedy administration's policy shift from "nuclear deterrence" to "planned nuclear stalemate," in which nuclear war is "unthinkable."[22] In Dodd's view, this policy shift implied the diminished willingness of the United States "to risk a thermonuclear war to cope with Soviet aggression." Dodd concluded that the development of the neutron bomb "would free Western Europe from the worrisome reliance on the unpredictable balance of thermonuclear terror, and from the alternative of having to oppose the far more numerous divisions of the Soviet bloc in Europe in a battle limited to conventional weapons."[23] In contrast to the objections of many Europeans that ERWs would relegate a nuclear conflict to devastation of their territory alone, Dodd claimed that the absence of significant fallout from ERWs "would reduce the political opposition of our allies to the use of TNWs and, to this extent, would make the resort to such weapons far more plausible."[24]

Arguments against the development of the neutron bomb in 1963 took the form of efforts to gain support for the test ban treaty. The Kennedy administration chose Adrian Fisher, then deputy director of the Arms Control and Disarmament Agency, to refute allegations by Senator Dodd that the development of the neutron bomb would "make attempts to set up a total nuclear test ban . . . meaningless since tests on . . . weapons of this type could

be concealed underground."[25] A fierce executive–legislative battle ensued, with Fisher representing the administration and Dodd the opinions of congressional opponents of the test ban. Fisher claimed that the chief interest of the United States in the neutron bomb was to prevent the Soviet Union and other countries from acquiring this kind of weapon. In Fisher's opinion, the neutron bomb "would not appear to constitute a great advantage to either side,"[26] a statement diametrically opposed to Dodd's claim that "the nation which first perfects . . . these weapons [neutron bomb and the anti-missile missile] will decisively overturn the balance of power."[27] In a letter to Senator Dodd, Fisher stressed that "an enhanced radiation weapon of a type now available"[28] might increase the risk of escalation from tactical to strategic nuclear conflict. He therefore concluded that existing fission weapons were sufficient for deterrence and that "an inhibition to the development of fusion weapons would be to our net advantage."[29]

Despite vigorous objections by the armed services, the Partial Test Ban Treaty was passed by the Senate and signed by President Kennedy in 1963.[30] Battlefield nuclear weapons were a low priority during the mid-60s, but the enhanced radiation concept was tested in various strategic roles. An enhanced radiation capability was designed and tested for the Sprint ballistic missile, a component of the Sentinel ABM (antiballistic missile) defense system developed for the U.S. Army. But the project was heavily criticized by both Congress and portions of the military and was finally canceled in 1969, primarily because the ABM system on the whole was deemed ineffective, excessively costly, and militarily provocative. The Sprint missile then became a component of a new ABM defense project called Safeguard. The project was supported by the Nixon administration and approved by Congress in 1969-70, boosted by the administration's claim that the ABM system would be a valuable "bargaining chip" in SALT negotiations. Safeguard was canceled as a result of the 1972 ABM treaty included in SALT I. Consequently, the U.S. Army lost the potentially large nuclear mission that ABMs would have provided, at a time when its other missions were being reduced as America withdrew from Vietnam. Moreover, Congress was exerting heavy pressure on the administration to reduce U.S. manpower levels in Europe. Several observers contend that the Army began to lobby the administration for an enhanced radiation battlefield weapon as a substitute for its declining conventional missions in Europe. Yet a number of senior Army leaders regarded ERWs as ineffective on the battlefield, based on controversial evidence that enemy troops would be instantly incapacitated only within a relatively small area near the explosion.

Attempts by the scientific community to adapt the enhanced radiation concept to viable weaponry continued throughout the 1960s, albeit at a moderate pace. In addition to their role in the ABM system, "radiation-enhanced" weapons were considered for battlefield deployment. In 1967

information from AEC reports on the status of this development became available:

> A major effort is underway to perfect small precise tactical nuclear warheads, including some that are practically free from fallout . . ."that could make nuclear weapons more useable in Europe" according to a top military planner. . . . Thus the major program to develop what one general called "cookie-cutter nuclear weapons." . . ."We're fast developing small warheads offering very precise predictable effects."[31]

Similar statements on ERW development reported that

> the AEC is conducting research on ERWs. Such a device would be very "clean." The term "very clean" would mean a device in which only a small amount of the energy released would come from fission. The blast effect would be very small, but the radiation effect from neutrons would be predominant. The AEC also is conducting research on pure fusion weapons. The status of programs for developing such weapons is classified.[32]

In 1973 the AEC, which had budget authority over the research and development of nuclear warheads, requested Congress to appropriate funds for the improvement of artillery fired atomic projectiles (AFAP), including the development of a new standard fission warhead. (The 155 mm and 8-inch artillery shells have been deployed in Europe with both nuclear and conventional warheads since the early 1960s.) The nuclear weapons labs had lobbied long and hard for replacing the AFAP's existing standard fission warhead with a neutron warhead. Dr. Harold Agnew, director of the Los Alamos Lab, told the JCAE: "We at Los Alamos are working very aggressively, trying to influence the DoD to consider using these [deleted] weapons which could be very decisive on a battlefield, yet would limit collateral damage that is usually associated with nuclear weapons."[33] The Army, however, preferred the higher-yield fission warheads. Furthermore, some senior civilian defense officials in the Pentagon were apparently already aware of the political sensitivities surrounding the neutron bomb. Having thus decided against requesting an enhanced radiation warhead for the artillery shells, the Pentagon and the AEC expected to have little difficulty in obtaining congressional approval for their production. The Joint Committee on Atomic Energy, however, refused to appropriate funds. The majority of the committee was disillusioned by the controversial arguments regarding the weapon's military effectiveness, certain to create problems with their eventual deployment in Europe, and by what were considered exorbitant costs. The reservations about their military utility concerned risks of two parallel sorts inherent in TNWs of any type placed close to NATO–Warsaw Pact borders. First, in a potential combat situation, TNWs so close to enemy forces might risk being overrun. A

related concern was the fear that their forward positioning would force a decision on their use far sooner than might be desirable or necessary. In general, the senators were not convinced that these weapons could be used in a limited nuclear conflict without forcing escalation to strategic nuclear weapons.[34] The second objection was the cost of the new nuclear shells. The cost of each shell was over $400,000 and the total request amounted to $1.3 billion,[35] although military spokesmen claimed that most or all of this cost could be defrayed by salvaging the nuclear material in the older shells that would be retired. Another major factor was the fervent opposition of Senator Symington, chairman of the subcommittee, to any further increases in the TNW stockpile, although there is no evidence that he was specifically opposed to ERWs. He was particularly concerned that the allies were not paying their fair share of the burden of collective defense and suggested that "our allies should take over much, if not most, of their own defense."[36] Moreover, he believed that the military sought to acquire all available weapons, even if a justifiable rationale for their development did not exist: "If there's no hold on the military they will ask for everything. . . ."[37] Under the previous chairman, Senator Jackson, the committee as a whole had been a promoter of more nuclear weapons, and the subcommittee had played an instrumental role in the late 1950s in pushing for thousands of TNWs. Thus a combination of factors—general objection to nuclear artillery, cost, and the influential role of Senator Symington—defeated the Army's request for modernized artillery warheads.

A number of senior Army leaders had previously opposed an enhanced radiation warhead for the new projectiles, owing to controversy over the radius at which a neutron blast would be militarily effective. They had expressed concern that ERWs might not simultaneously be able to incapacitate the desired number of enemy personnel and to limit collateral damage to the subsequent forward movement of NATO's second-echelon troops. The deployed higher-yield fission warheads met the Army's requirements for achieving specific damage goals. But with the rejection of its request for modernized nuclear artillery, the Army began to fear the erosion of a key nuclear mission. The drastic decline in nuclear-capable air defense forces had been followed by the negotiated abandonment in SALT I of the Army's ABM system, the service's best hope for a long-term nuclear role. There was talk in NATO forums and at the Mutual Balanced Force Reductions (MBFR) talks in Vienna of reducing the number of TNWs in Europe. Thus there were powerful institutional incentives for the Army to devise novel weapons that could protect its claim to a nuclear mission. Furthermore, shortly after Congress rejected the request for new fission warheads, Secretary of Defense James Schlesinger issued a directive instructing the Army to submit new proposals for the artillery projectiles. Subsequently, on August 29, 1973, the Army's chief of staff initiated a study to "reexamine" nuclear warhead requirements for

artillery projectiles.[38] This study, whose requirements included the minimization of collateral damage, established the Army's incentive for pursuing development of the neutron warhead.

During the 1973 congressional hearings on the modernization of nuclear artillery, General Goodpaster, then Supreme Allied Commander, Europe made clear that one of the criteria for enhancing the credibility of TNWs was political acceptability in NATO's employment planning process.[39] Yet these hearings also illuminate the lack of allied consensus on TNWs. West Germany was apparently disturbed by the proposals for new low-yield weapons, evidenced by a warning given to Senator Symington by the AEC on this matter: "Please don't discuss it with him [Chancellor Brandt] at all; it is a very sensitive subject."[40] A report issued by the Senate Foreign Relations Committee late in 1973 expounded on the unresolved nuclear issues in NATO, the very issues that formed the crux of the controversy over ERWs:

> European concern was stimulated by press stories during the course of the past year that the United States had developed or was developing a new generation of tactical nuclear weapons which combined low and variable yield possibilities with *enhanced radiation* characteristics and which could be used with dual capable artillery. . . .
>
> Knowledge of the possibility of the development of this technology has given rise to a number of concerns within NATO. Most Europeans fear that the deployment of mini-nukes could significantly lower the nuclear threshold, although some would apparently like to see mini-nukes developed and deployed as replacements for certain weapons in the existing U.S. inventory in Europe, an inventory which even senior U.S. officials acknowledge includes many older weapons of unnecessarily high yield. Apparently some Europeans also believe that the deployment of mini-nukes would lead to reduction in conventional forces.
>
> Some Europeans expressed the view . . . that the United States was not being responsive on the subject of mini-nukes. Although U.S. military officers . . . definitely favor their development and deployment, some officials at NATO said that, in their view, the United States has thus far sought *to avoid serious discussion of the issue* using the rationale that U.S. policy and law precludes the discussion of new weapons before deployment is a practical possibility.
>
> There is a considerable gap between the desires of the U.S. military with regard to the deployment of mini-nukes and the German Government's understanding of those views. . . .
>
> The German Government's publicly stated positions on mini-nukes and ADMs [atomic demolition munitions] indicate considerable ambivalence on the subject of tactical nuclear weapons. While the Germans are naturally interested in weapons that minimize collateral damage, they are also acutely sensitive to the possibility that the introduction of "smaller, cleaner" weapons could blur the line dividing conventional from nuclear weapons and could

mean that nuclear weapons would be used earlier with the danger that this could lead to an escalatory process. At his July 22 press conference Defense Minister Leber said with regard to ADMs: "The first use of nuclear weapons would mean a change in the kind of war being fought, and one should really not draw important distinctions between the various kinds of nuclear weapons." In the same press conference Leber also said that even the use of a "single atomic hand grenade" would cause escalation to the most powerful nuclear weapons.[41] [Emphasis added.]

Several months later a former Bundeswehr general complained about the lack of dialogue between the United States and its allies: "Until now thoughts about a new approach to the use of very small nuclear weapons have been kept under the carpet." At the same time he issued a warning to his fellow Europeans:

> No decision has been made even to produce these new weapons, and recently one has heard from America that they do not intend to. That is how it stands today, but I am sure one should not exclude the possibility that one fine day we Europeans will be presented with the arrival of these weapons. . . . We should firmly recognise that this would constitute what should be described without exaggeration as a revolution in nuclear weapons technique, a revolution which, whether we like it or not, will impose its effects on us faster and faster.[42]

Unfortunately, his prescience was not heeded.

Yet some of the issues of TNW modernization had been raised, at least in general terms, at meetings of NATO's Nuclear Planning Group (NPG) in 1973. The communiques of these classified meetings refer to the neutron bomb only once, and then only indirectly: "The United States is developing a new 8-inch nuclear projectile with greater accuracy and much reduced collateral damage." The communiques imply that the allies did not on the whole disapprove of the modernization program, but the brief public statements do not reveal the positions of individual countries. At an allied conference in Paris in May 1973 the United States informed the allies that the new TNWs could be ready for deployment in Europe in 3 to 5 years. The first public European responses appeared after this conference, most of them negative. The European press viewed the new developments as reflecting the American proclivity to capitalize on technological advances for their own sake, without sufficient attention to the full range of political and military ramifications. One such response came from Lord Chalfont in an article entitled "Time to Shoot Down the Pentagon's Latest Bit of Gee-Whizzery."[43] Much of the press predicted that European defense chiefs were likely to oppose the new low-yield warheads.[44]

The substantive concern of the Europeans was over the rationales for employment of short-range, low-yield nuclear weapons designed for use on their battlefields. The doctrinal ambiguity in flexible response had permitted the opposing logics of TNW employment to go unresolved. The basis of

European criticism was derived from a different set of considerations than those of American opponents of the new weapons. The American arms control community felt that these weapons would lower the nuclear threshold, leading to a greater possibility of initiation of use and subsequent retaliation. The Europeans feared just the opposite: that the weapons implied "a reduced US nuclear commitment" to the defense of Europe with strategic nuclear weapons, leaving them with neither nuclear deterrence nor conventional defense. Given that American officials were now admitting that "as time goes on, and with approximate strategic parity, . . . the value of the nuclear umbrella may be reduced,"[45] the United States was trying to develop the "principle of the intermediate option between conventional warfare and strategic nuclear exchange."[46] This intermediate option includes the use of low-yield, discriminate nuclear weapons to fight a limited nuclear war, which Europe fears above all else, as it is thought to cause at least as many casualties as conventional warfare and simultaneously decouple the use of TNWs in Europe from the U.S. strategic nuclear deterrent. Even a spokesman for the Energy Research and Development Administration (ERDA), the successor to the AEC, stressed that

> Our allies find themselves on the horn of a dilemma in that conventional warfare within their country would create as many casualties as these small nuclear weapons will create. . . . Our allies are therefore faced by the dilemma in considering the use of nuclear weapons. What we are suggesting here is that technology can provide a sharpened nuclear sword with a lot less attendent casualties but certainly not without casualties. It is *impossible* to fight such a war.[47] [Emphasis added]

Thus there was a latent uneasiness within the Alliance over whether highly accurate, low-yield nuclear weapons, which can potentially reduce casualties to that of conventional warfare, were a desirable enhancement to NATO's tactical nuclear arsenal. Europe wanted "usable" nuclear weapons to imply the highest possible degree of escalation, whereas the United States recognized "that those that carry the highest escalatory effect are the ones that we would be the most reluctant to use."[48] If a limited conflict cannot be contained, Europe wants to be certain that the United States will escalate the conflict to the strategic realm, thereby diverting excessive casualties and massive destruction from its territory. In 1973 the United States appeared to be hedging its risks, reluctant to guarantee that its strategic nuclear forces would remain indefinitely coupled to limited tactical nuclear use. The words of General Goodpaster, SACEUR, were certainly not taken lightly by Europeans: "The notion of an automatic and certain connection [between tactical and strategic nuclear weapons], such that any use would certainly be followed by use at the full-scale—that concept of coupling . . . goes too far."[49]

The irreconcilable nature of American and European rationales for TNW employment policy made modernization a sensitive issue within the Alliance. If the doctrinal dilemmas could not be satisfactorily resolved, TNW modernization would have to proceed cautiously, with much attention to the political, as well as military, consequences of change. Schlesinger stressed this point in his 1975 report to Congress: "It is vital . . . that the *process of change* be recognized as equal in importance to the changes themselves, so that the military posture is improved while maintaining the political cohesiveness of NATO."[50] [Emphasis added.] The importance of the "process of change" hinges on the central issue of commitment, which seemed, to Europe, to be threatened by the introduction of low-yield, reduced-collateral-damage TNWs that would diminish the escalatory effects of their employment. In 1975 Schlesinger explained some of the ramifications of the modernization program:

> U.S. TNF deployed in Europe have been for years a major symbol of the earnest U.S. commitment to the common defense of the Alliance. Consequently, possible changes in the TNF posture must be carefully evaluated from the military perspective and with an eye to the message these changes convey to the Allies and adversaries about the future U.S. commitment to this common defense.
>
> These political and psychological considerations must be taken fully into account in any assessment of the U.S. nuclear posture in Europe and in determining whether adjustments in that posture are desirable. . . . There must be full consultation with the Allies in both the military and political deliberations that could lead to any changes in posture.[51]

Considerations of this sort were not addressed in the first several months of the 1977 debate on ERWs.

In November 1976 President Ford signed a bill approving a request by the Energy Research and Development Administration to fund research and development of ERWs. Public testimoney on ERW development began in early 1977 when General Bratton, an ERDA spokesman, reported to the House Committee on Armed Services:

> Systems now under development include . . . the W70 mod 3 Lance ERW, . . . the W79 8-inch Artillery Fired Atomic Projectile and . . . an improved replacement for the existing W48 155 mm artillery shell. . . .
>
> Advanced development is the essential source of new concepts needed to maintain the quality of the U.S. nuclear weapons deterrent.[52]

At the time ERDA's request was approved, NATO had still not resolved its differences over the rationales for TNWs. But by 1977 the organizational and political impediments that had prevented the application of enhanced radiation technology to viable weapons systems had weakened. Earlier

resistance within some sections of the Army had been transformed into strong support. The chairman of the Senate Subcommittee on Military Applications, Stuart Symington, who had ardently opposed TNW modernization, was no longer in the Senate. As Graham Allison and Frederic Morris have observed, "In the usual case, a new weapon has 'simmered on the back burner,' ignored or denounced, before it reaches the battlefield. Often, only the pressures of combat and the revolutionary zeal of iconoclastic sponsors overcome official skepticism and hostility so as to give the weapon a chance."[53] The United States was now ready to give ERWs a chance. But the issues of deterrence and defense, escalation and limited nuclear war were still "simmering on the back burner" in NATO. A little prodding from the press opened the Pandora's box.

NOTES

1. Quoted in Sam Cohen, *The Truth About the Neutron Bomb: The Inventor of the Bomb Speaks Out* (New York: William Morrow, 1983) p. 48.

2. Fred M. Kaplan, "Enhanced-Radiation Weapons," *Scientific American* 238 (May 1978): 46-47.

3. Cohen, p. 137.

4. Ibid., p. 44.

5. George B. Kistiakowsky, "Enhanced Radiation Warheads, Alias the Neutron Bomb," *Technology Review*, May 1978, p. 24.

6. Edward Gemarekian, "New A-Bomb 'Pinpoints' Lethal Dose," Washington *Post*, July 19, 1959, p. 1.

7. Cohen, p. 64.

8. Letter from Senator Dodd to President-elect Kennedy, November 25, 1960, quoted in ibid., pp. 69-71.

9. Letter from Senator Dodd to President Kennedy, April 7, 1961, quoted in ibid., pp. 73-74.

10. Cohen, p. 82.

11. Ibid., p. 83.

12. Ibid., p. 84.

13. Ibid., p. 85.

14. U.S. Congress, Senate, Senator Dodd, *Congressional Record*, February 21, 1963. p. 2804.

15. Ibid.

16. Ibid.

17. Ibid.

18. Ibid., p. 2805.

19. *Congressional Record*, April 9, 1963, p. 5989.

20. *Congressional Record*, March 7, 1963, p. 3633.

21. *Congressional Record*, February 21, 1963, p. 2805.

22. Ibid., Senator Dodd, p. 2806, and Senator Thurmond, p. 2837; John F. Loosbrock, "Strategic Retreat from Reality," *Air Force Magazine*, January 1963, reprinted in *Congressional Record*, February 21, 1963, pp. 2825-27.

23. Senator Dodd, *Congressional Record*, February 21, 1963, p. 2806.

24. *Congressional Record*. April 9, 1963, p. 5989.

25. Washington *Post*, May 12, 1960.

26. *Congressional Record*, April 9, 1963, p. 5989.

27. Letter to the Washington *Post* by Senator Dodd, March 1, 1963.

28. *Congressional Record*, April 9, 1963, p. 5986.

29. Ibid.

30. President Kennedy had sought a Comprehensive Test Ban with the Soviets but was unable to convince two-thirds of the Senate to support him. It was Senator Dodd who both led the fight against the Comprehensive Test Ban and eventually enabled Kennedy to obtain Senate ratification of the Partial Test Ban Treaty. Dodd, a Democrat who had earned the wrath of a Democratic administration as a result of his battle against the treaty, was up for reelection in 1964, as was Kennedy. Sensing that his opposition to the Comprehensive Test Ban would hurt him at the polls in liberal Connecticut, he struck a deal with Senator Hubert Humphrey, who was displeased with Dodd for his opposition to the treaty, to cosponsor a resolution to offer the Soviets an agreement to ban all nuclear tests in the atmoshpere and underwater. The Dodd-Humphrey Resolution led to U.S.-Soviet agreement on and Senate ratification of the Partial Test Ban Treaty, which banned nuclear tests in space, in the air, and underwater.

31. William Beecher, "'Clean' Warheads Sought for NATO," New York *Times*, May 20, 1967, p. 1.

32. Baltimore *Sun*, September 1968, quoted on Claude Witze, "The Wayward Press: Fallout from the Neutron Bomb," *Air Force Magazine* 60 (November 1977): 20.

33. *Military Applications of Nuclear Technology*, Hearings before the Subcommittee on Military Applications of Nuclear Technology of the Joint Committee on Atomic Energy, 93rd Cong., 1st sess., 1973, pt. 1 p. 49.

34. Senator Stuart Symington, ibid., p. 37.

35. *Military Applications of Nuclear Technology*, pt. 2, p. 101.

36. Ibid., p. 54.

37. Ibid., pt. 1, p. 54.

38. Cohen, p. 100.

39. *Military Applications of Nuclear Technology*, pt. 2, p. 65.

40. Ibid.

41. U.S. Congress, Subcommittee on U.S. Security Agreements and Commitments Abroad of the Senate Committee on Foreign Relations, *Report on U.S. Security Issues in Europe: Burden Sharing and Offset, MBFR and Nuclear Weapons*, 93rd Cong., 1st sess., pp. 22-23, December 2, 1973.

42. General J. A. Graf Kielmansegg, "A German View of Western Defense," *RUSI Journal*, March 1974, p. 15.

43. *Times* (London), May 14, 1973.

44. C. Douglas Home, *Times* (London), May 7, 1973.

45. Major General Edward B. Giller, USAF, *Military Applications of Nuclear Technology*, June 29, 1973, pt. 1, p. 34.

46. Dr. Carl Walske, ibid., pt. 2, pp. 48-49.

47. Maj. Gen. Giller, ibid., pt.1, pp. 34, 36.

48. General A. J. Goodpaster, ibid., pt. 2, p. 120.

49. Ibid.

50. James R. Schlesinger, *The Theater Nuclear Force Posture in Europe, A Report to the U.S. Congress*, April 1975, quoted in *Nuclear Strategy and National Security: Points of View*, Robert J. Pranger and Roger P. Labrie, eds.(Washington, D.C.: American Enterprise Institute for Public Policy Research, 1977), p. 169.

51. Ibid., pp. 169, 186.

52. U.S. Congress, *Hearings before the House Armed Services Committee on H.R. 6566, ERDA Authorization Legislation (National Security Programs) for Fiscal Year 1978*, 95th Cong., 1st sess., 1977, pp. 36, 196.

53. Graham T. Allison and Frederic A. Morris, "Precision Guidance for NATO: Justification and Constraints," in *Beyond Nuclear Deterrence: New Aims, New Arms*, Johan J. Holst and Uwe Nerlich, eds. (London: Macdonald and Jane's, 1977), p. 208.

3

A Crisis Develops
in the United States

This chapter examines the beginning of the neutron bomb controversy in the United States. The time is June to early September 1977. The chapter addresses the following questions: How did ERWs become a political issue and how did the American government approach the issue? Who was involved and how did they perceive their involvement? The actions and attitudes of American officials are accurately characterized by Richard Neustadt's phrase: "Foreign Relations begin at home."[1] The way in which American officials perceived the issues is crucial to any understanding of why ERWs provoked a controversy over decision making within NATO.

The role of the press and its influence on governmental decisions and actions is a pervasive part of the controversy. The press brought the neutron bomb to the attention of the American and allied government officials who participated in the resolution of the crisis and thus played a major role in shaping the views of the participants.

The role of Congress was to establish the range of action available to the administration by defining the domestic political constraints. The narrow margin by which Congress approved funds for ERWs was an indication to the administration that it would need to build a wide domestic consensus to gain backing for its policy. Congress was also instrumental in casting the federal bureaucracies into adversarial roles with one another. Pressure from Congress to get an Arms Control Impact Statement that would reflect the administration's overall view of the weapon's impact on ongoing arms control negotiations pitted the Arms Control and Disarmament Agency against the Department of Defense and the National Security Council.

Domestic political considerations and personal convictions were influential in shaping the views of the president and foreign policy and national security bureaucracies. Carter's difficulty in adopting a firm position on the neutron bomb resulted from the need to take into account the numerous and often divergent pressures that converged upon him once the weapon became an object of public scrutiny. The president's particularly equivocal view of nuclear weapons reinforced his reluctancee to take a definite stand on the issue. Carter's determination to establish an approach to foreign policy that would be significantly different from the Kissinger era was a decisive factor in shaping the president's perspective on how to handle the issues. In his opinion, a more pluralistic approach to Alliance decision making would not only differentiate his foreign policy from that of the previous administration but would also alleviate some of the burdens associated with nuclear decisions. Moreover, building a consensus within NATO on production and deployment of the neutron bomb was an appealing way to avoid a major domestic row with Congress.

The administration's approach to the issue reveals a common facet of alliance relations: misperception. The administration's lack of sensitivity to European concerns was due to muddled perceptions of the allies' own domestic political constraints. Misperception was compounded by a generational change within the American foreign policy establishment.

THE NEUTRON BOMB MEDIA EVENT

The press played a major role in the neutron bomb controversy. In a sense, the press made the neutron bomb a political issue. Without exposure by the press, ERWs probably would have been funded without debate by Congress and deployed in Europe with perhaps only minimal private consultation between allied leaders. The information that appeared in the American press in early June 1977 shaped all the future participants' views of the issues involved and the action that should be taken.

Each participant saw a different face of the issue in the press reports, depending on the particular concerns of his profession. For Congress, it was a matter of investigating why this weapon had passed unnoticed through the budgetary process. For ACDA, it was a matter of assessing the weapon's impact on ongoing arms control negotiations. For the Defense Department, the task was to prove that this weapon should be funded by Congress and deployed in Europe. The State Department saw the weapon in terms of its impact on Alliance relations. In addition to its military utility, the weapon had to be politically acceptable to allied governments. The National Security Council had to coordinate the views of all the bureaucracies and organize a course of action that was consistent with the president's views. The president himself

had to take all these factors—budget, arms control, defense, and foreign relations—into account, weigh them against his own personal foreign policy and national security objectives and his political instincts, and make a decision that would be as consistent as possible with all these considerations. The information on which all these participants' views were based was heavily influenced by the way in which the press presented the issues.

Like the participants in government, the reporter who wrote the first article on ERWs in June 1977 had his own personal interests and convictions to advance. The beginning of a crisis in Alliance relations, the so-called neutron bomb controversy, can be traced to June 6, 1977, when the Washington *Post* published an article by Walter Pincus entitled "Neutron Killer Warhead Buried in ERDA Budget." Pincus had worked for Senator Symington as staff assistant to the Joint Committee on Atomic Energy during the first hearings on the modernization of nuclear artillery in 1973. Despite the contentious issues raised in the earlier hearings, the press had not given them much attention. Pincus had written articles opposing TNWs in general several years ago. His coverage of ERWs, for which he won the Raymond Clapper Award for excellence in reporting, clearly reflected his conviction that "nuclear artillery is dangerous as a concept."[2] Pincus saw the neutron bomb as an opportunity to expound both his personal convictions and his belief that the public was being deceived by officials about the substantive issues involved in the decision. One official charged that "he was interested in blocking development and production of the weapons and he wanted to put it in the worst possible light."[3]

Pincus's description suggested that ERWs were uniquely pernicious among TNWs and that the Pentagon had deliberately attempted to conceal its appropriation request from Congress. Pincus referred to the neutron bomb as the "first nuclear battlefield weapon specially designed to kill people through the release of neutrons rather than to destroy military installations through heat and blast."[4] These weapons, he continued, would inflict singularly dreadful injuries, whose symptoms include "convulsions, intermittent stupor and lack of muscle coordination. Death is certain in a few hours to several days."[5] This allegation revealed a real disagreement between the weapon's military proponents and Pincus, for he doubted the weapon's ability to limit collateral effects and long-term radiation damage to a relatively small area. Pincus accurately, albeit in a sensational manner, described the weapon's effects based on a study produced by the Atomic Energy Commission. He cleverly employed phraseology used by officials in earlier hearings—such as "the real estate bomb" and "destroys people and leaves buildings intact"—to underscore his opposition to the weapon. Pincus was technically correct, since the weapons military advantages are characterized by the increased capability to inflict damage upon troops, as opposed to their equipment. Nevertheless, the counterposing of people and military installations suggested the bombing of cities or factories rather than defending against a massed tank force. Other

aspects of the coverage revealed the same willingness to imply questionable results. The Washington *Post* repeatedly used the phrase "KILLER WARHEAD" in headlines over the following weeks, and on one occasion Pincus used it in the lead of a story. One supporter of the weapon claimed that Pincus and the *Post* produced a series of misleading "killer warhead" headlines, employed sensationalism, and exaggerated various aspects of the story.[6] This phrase was finally dropped after some supporters of the weapon held a meeting with *Post* editors.

But the impact on public opinion had already been made. On July 7 a group of demonstrators, after an overnight vigil, flung vials of blood at the Pentagon to protest the weapon.[7] Papers across the country were flooded with "Letters to the Editor," almost all of them opposed to the weapons. One letter charged that the ERW "insults our dignity as humanitarians by subordinating the values of human life to the spoils of war." "American deeds at Hiroshima and in Vietnam rivaled Hitler's gas ovens for cold-blooded cruelty," another letter proclaimed, "with the neutron weapons, we may have the capacity to outdo him." Other comments branded it "a startling new concept in genocide," and "inhuman forms of weaponry." Clearly, these types of responses could have been directed against any form of nuclear weaponry, not only the ERW. As Bernard Weinraub wrote in the New York *Times*: "What seems to have emerged out of the confusion and emotive rhetoric surrounding the neutron bomb—some reports have referred to the neutron weapons as a "killer warhead" as if there were some other kind—is a tense debate about nuclear war itself and the use of nuclear weapons."[8]

The same sort of rhetoric was used by leading American officials: in mid-July UN Ambassador Andrew Young told reporters that "it doesn't make sense to spend all that money killing folks."[9] Perhaps more significant was the misleading context into which arguments by professional military critics were placed. Herbert Scoville, former Department of Defense official and deputy director of the CIA, made a cogent case against the ERW's military effectiveness in the New York *Times* on July 12. He argued that the radiation dose of the proposed ERWs was not large enough instantly to incapacitate the enemy, thereby conceivably allowing enemy troops to fight on for several days. This criticism was not new, as the Army itself had earlier expressed a similar reservation. However a cursory reading of Scoville's article was most likely to elicit emotional abhorrence rather than reasoned opinion. A line from the article—"Neutron bombs have been proclaimed the 'supercapitalist weapon,' preserving property while killing and sickening people"—was quoted in large bold type in the middle of the page. Above was a depiction of this sentence: a skeleton holding a "neutron bomb," standing in the corridor of an undamaged building. This sort of "yellow journalism" undoubtedly had a significant impact on the future course of events and on the president's decision.

The attack on the neutron bomb was not limited to exaggerations or emotional descriptions of the weapon itself: Pincus and the Washington *Post*

implied that the Pentagon had been dishonest in its presentation to Congress and the White House. Pincus's claim that the appropriation request was "buried" in the ERDA public works bill suggested that the defense community had made a deliberate effort to conceal the proposals from both Congress and the public. Pincus later claimed that since many of the specific references to ERWs had been deleted from unclassified versions of earlier hearings, neither the public nor most of Congress were aware of the issues involved.[10] Yet public testimony on ERWs had taken place and was available to the general public, as the above record indicates. But the wording of Pincus's article seemed to charge ERDA with purposeful illegal actions. Shortly after the article appeared, Alton Frye, of the Council on Foreign Relations, wrote: "The disreputable procedures through which the weapons nearly evaded legal and public scrutiny may prejudice one's initial view of the case."[11] In response, one observer remarked that "had the Pentagon wished to 'bury' the weapon, it would have resorted to the usual technique in such cases, and lumped it in the "miscellaneous category."[12] Actually, Pincus's article revealed nothing either deliberately concealed or extraordinarily new about ERWs to Congress or the American public.

The only serious revelation in the spate of articles on ERWs concerned the president's awareness of the proposals. In late June the Washington *Post* wrote: "But wait a minute, President Ford, it seems, was at best minimally briefed before he let money for neutron warhead production slip into the budget stream."[13] Yet just the previous day Pincus had written that President Ford "knew the concept and application of enhanced radiation to these weapons when he made the production decision."[14] But whether President Carter knew what was in the budget approved by President Ford is still open to question. Just two weeks after the first article appeared, when the Senate was in the midst of a heated debate over whether to fund ERDA's request for ERWs, Carter asked Congress to approve the proposal in case he chose to proceed with production. White House spokesmen claimed that the president was reviewing the proposal, a review that continued until September 1977, by which time Alliance relations had steadily deteriorated and tremendous public opposition was mounting in Europe.

THE CONGRESSIONAL DEBATES

Meanwhile, the U.S. Congress turned its attention to the neutron bomb, which had become a matter of concern only with the publication of Pincus's article and the subsequent flurry of activity. The congressional debates are significant because they focused on the domestic political concerns that were important to executive action. Congress serves as an important forum for the discussion of national interests and priorities that must be taken into account in any executive decision on foreign policy or national security. In the neutron

bomb controversy, Congress played an instrumental role in weighing the arguments and making vital decisions on funding. Because the legislative branch had the authority to approve funds for the research and development of ERWs, Congress made the administration aware of the domestic political constraints that needed to be considered in the president's decision. If the Congress had not approved funds for the ERWs, the scope of presidential action would have been severely curtailed. The narrow margin by which Congress approved funds for ERWs was an indication to the administration that it would need to build a wide domestic consensus to gain backing for its policy. In addition to winning Congress's approval for a decision on the neutron bomb, Carter would have to think about his overall influence and long-term relations with Congress. If a large portion of Congress disapproved of his actions in this event, the president's ability to win support for other policies and programs might be jeopardized.

Congress's approval of funds for ERWs was not taken without severe reservation. On June 14 the House approved ERDA's fiscal year 1978 public works bill, which included funds for the development of ERWs.[15] Eight days later the Senate Appropriations Committee approved production funds for the Lance ERW, defeating 10-10 an amendment by Senator Mark Hatfield to delete such funding until the president had decided to proceed with the program, at which point Congress would make the final decision.[16] Hatfield led the Senate opposition to the neutron bomb. He opposed its production for two reasons, one procedural, the other substantive: First, he vehemently objected to Carter's repeated requests that Congress should approve funds for the weapon before the president had decided to support its production and deployment in Europe. Second, he was convinced that deployment of neutron warheads would lower the threshold for nuclear war—making a nuclear confrontation more likely. A limited nuclear war initiated by the use of these weapons in a conventional conflict would precipitate the use of larger atomic weapons.[17]

On July 1 the Senate held a closed session on the neutron bomb in order to discuss at length the military implications of the weapon. After two and a half hours, the Senate resumed in open session and quickly moved to vote on an amendment by Senator Stennis to an amendment proposed by Senator Hatfield. Hatfield's amendment proposed "that none of the funds appropriated in this or any other Act shall be used for production of ERWs."[18] Stennis's amendment modified Hatfield's proposition by delaying funds "until an Arms Control Impact Statement has been filed with Congress and the President certifies to Congress that these weapons are in the national interest."[19] By a one-vote margin, the Senate voted 43-42 in favor of the Stennis amendment, in effect a vote against the Hatfield amendment.

The Missing ACIS

Congress was also instrumental in casting the federal bureaucracies into adversarial roles with one another. Pressure from Congress to get an Arms Control Impact Statement (ACIS) that would reflect the administration's overall view of the weapon's impact on ongoing arms control negotiations pitted the Arms Control and Disarmament Agency against the Department of Defense (DoD) and the National Security Council (NSC): ACDA was interested in promoting its credibility as an essential link in the processes of arms control and weapons acquisition; the Pentagon, supported by the NSC, wanted to move forward with its defense programs. The Senate's demand for an ACIS on the Lance ERW brought ACDA into the deliberations on the neutron bomb as a full-fledged participant. If ACDA had not been allowed a regularized channel of influence, the implications of arms control considerations might have been deliberately ignored by other bureaucracies who viewed such considerations as a hindrance to the weapon's political acceptability both within the United States and with the allies.

Arms Control Impact Statements were a recent addition to the weapons acquisition process. In November 1975 President Ford had signed into law a bill that for the first time sought to legislate a specific arms control input into the executive defense budgetary process. The bill requires that any government agency requesting authorization or appropriations from Congress for any program of research and development, or modernization, relating to nuclear armaments or to programs with a total or annual cost in excess of $250 million or $50 million, respectively, accompany such requests with a statement analyzing the program's impact on arms control and disarmament policy and negotiations. In its initial hearings on the neutron bomb, the Senate discovered that no ACIS had been submitted for the Lance enhanced radiation warhead. On June 23 Senator Claiborne Pell, chairman of the Senate Foreign Relations Subcommittee on Arms Control, requested that Paul Warnke, the director of ACDA, coordinate the preparation of an ACIS for this weapons program.[20]

This request set off the first round of bureaucratic in-fighting that would characterize the politics of ERWs. As an attempt to force the executive branch to regularize and systematize an arms control input into defense programs, particularly nuclear weapons systems, ACIS had been, from its inception, viewed with skepticism by bureaucrats whose job it was to devise and implement defense programs. The State Department had expressed doubts about the ability of the legislation to have any effective impact on arms control policy. The Office of Management and Budget had actively opposed the legislation, not wanting yet another bureaucratic layer interposed in the defense budgetary process. ERDA and the Pentagon also adamantly opposed the ACIS process. The Defense Department, as Senator Hubert Humphrey remarked, was "not exactly singing the Hallelujah Chorus when this was

proposed."[21] "ACDA has no business, legally or otherwise, interfering with defense programs," protested a Pentagon official.[22] ACIS caused officials to view ACDA as an agent of Congress, menacing with DoD's traditional sovereignty over "its" budget. The Pentagon resented an outsider's poaching on its exclusive preserve of the armed services.[23]

The ACIS legislation directed both ACDA and the department requesting funds to draft statements on the arms control impact of that particular program. The NSC was assigned the crucial role of adjudicating between the various drafts and completing the final statement. By requiring NSC certification, the statements satisfied ACDA's demand that ACIS be an administration document, rather than an ACDA creation. Legislators had hoped that a process of interagency review coordinated by the NSC would not only enhance the credibility of the statements within the executive branch but would also avoid casting ACDA into an overt adversarial role with other agencies. But during the first two years of the ACIS process, fiscal years 1977 and 1978, ACDA was so viewed. Authors of the legislation soon realized that in order to avoid interagency squabbling the NSC might dilute or gut the entire procedure. Neither DoD nor ERDA wanted to admit that its defense programs had arms control liabilities. Thus the first set of ACISs produced by ERDA and DoD did not even mention the arms control implications of the weapons, but rather concentrated on a technical "program analysis."

Consequently the ACIS process was unenthusiastically undertaken by the Ford administration. Only 16 programs were covered, the statements averaged four sentences each, and all were classified.[24] DoD and ERDA each prepared a statement for the 8-inch nuclear artillery shell but enhanced radiation features were not mentioned. ACDA officials refused to participate because they felt they lacked the necessary guidelines and information on the weapons to draft substantive statements.[25] ACDA officials accused the Pentagon of denying them access to vital information on the weapons programs. ACDA began to view the process as more of an irritant and waste of time than as a procedure that served the cause of arms control.[26]

The ACIS process never acquired credibility under the Ford administration, according to one State Department official. The first set of ACISs were submitted in August 1976 for fiscal year 1977, after Congress had authorized the budget for that fiscal year. The Senate Foreign Relations Committee considered the procedure a charade and a disaster. Committee Chairman Sparkman and Senator Case wrote to Defense Secretary Rumsfeld, complaining that the ACISs "do not comply with the law and are unacceptable."[27] Nevertheless, no attempt was made by Congress to hold back appropriations for the programs in question.

For the fiscal year 1978 programs, 26 statements were submitted, 16 of which were merely resubmitted from the year before. They were drafted in late 1976 by the Ford administration, but this time an unclassified version was made available. Three of the statements concerned ERWs:

XM-785 improved 155 mm nuclear projectile
XM-753 improved 8-inch nuclear projectile
W-79 warhead for the XM-753[28]

When Congress reviewed these statements in April 1977 it again judged them unsatisfactory: They were too short and did not address the appropriate questions. The Senate Committee on Foreign Relations and the House Committee on International Relations requested the Congressional Research Service (CRS) to prepare a set of model ACISs. The evaluations by CRS were by and large critical, pointing out the large number of questions and considerations that had been omitted in the original text. The analysis of the W-79 (ERW) warhead suggested that if further testing of these warheads was necessary, such testing might impede possibilities for a Comprehensive Test Ban, which President Carter had proposed in a press interview on January 24, 1977. All the materials were made public in April 1977, evoking no congressional or press response.

Arms control advocates in the new Carter administration were anxious to give the ACIS process a sense of credibility it had lacked under the previous administration. In its first year, those involved in arms control in ACDA and the State Department saw the ACIS process as proof of their commitment to arms control. ACDA officials were driven by two requirements: to fulfill the request of Congress for adequate and substantial information on the arms control impact of all new weapons systems and to prove to themselves that arms control considerations could be successfully incorporated into the weapons acquisition process. ACDA officials stressed that this latter concern was as important to them as the legal requirement.

When Congress took up the neutron bomb issue in June, it requested provision of the ACISs pertaining to ERWs. In its initial review, the Senate Foreign Relations Committee discovered that no ACIS had been submitted for the Lance ERW. Congressional opponents of the weapons claimed that the administration was deliberately trying to conceal the issues involved. Although the omission was more a result of bureaucratic opposition to the ACIS process than a veiled attempt to avoid public debate on ERWs, the flurry of uncoordinated activity that followed gave Congress and the European allies reason to take a jaundiced view of the administration's proposal for these weapons.

Why was the ACIS on the Lance ERW not received by Congress in early 1977 along with those for the 8-inch and 155 mm nuclear projectiles? ACDA officials had drafted an ACIS for the Lance ERW in late 1976 as part of the fiscal year 1978 statements. Yet when it was circulated to DoD and ERDA for comment, this particular statement never emerged from the interagency review process. In the Defense Department, the office responsible for reviewing ACDA's draft of the impact statements was that of the assistant to the

secretary of defense for atomic energy, Dr. James Wade. Wade was, in principle, opposed to the ACIS procedure on the grounds that it impeded the process of weapons modernization by demanding scrutiny of weapons proposals by, what were in his view, unqualified individuals. In 1975 Wade had testified that the ACIS process was an unwarranted intrusion into the weapons acquisition process, that it would be time-consuming, burdensome, and costly.[29] When Wade received ACDA's draft of the ACIS for the Lance ERW in late 1976 he was troubled by its critical assessment of the weapon's arms control impact. He complained to Fred Iklé, then director of ACDA, and they agreed not to submit this statement. Wade claimed that this ACIS was not required because the appropriation request concerned only modernization of the existing warhead by enhanced radiation features, not a new weapon system. Iklé himself was not an avid supporter of the ACIS process. When the authorizing legislation had first been proposed in 1975, Iklé had objected to its potential to create an adversarial relationship between ACDA and other departments. In 1977 Iklé was not interested in becoming involved in an interagency dispute over ground support nuclear systems, such as the Lance, when his primary interest was in SALT, whose difficult negotiations were then threatening to divide the administration. An official familiar with the events later commented that the mutual agreement to withhold this impact statement was an effort "to duck the issue because the process was complicated and tedious." Apparently, the NSC, which was responsible for coordinating the statement, concurred with the agreement between Wade and Iklé, or at least did not question the omission. The failure to provide an ACIS for the Lance warhead was not a deliberate attempt to conceal the enhanced radiation concept from Congress; the other ACISs submitted to Congress had managed to assess the weapon while deleting references to enhanced radiation in the unclassified version. Most bureaucrats simply found ACIS an irksome procedure that complicated relations between the various departments.

When Senator Pell requested the administration to submit the missing ACIS immediately, ACDA officials viewed the request as a test of the agency's ability to make the ACIS process work. Carter had recently signed a presidential directive expanding the guidelines for drafting ACIS. ACDA officials drafted a new statement for the Lance ERW according to the new detailed standards for analysis, based on the critical evaluation by CRS. Because of the proliferation of information on ERWs in the media, ACDA officials were now well informed on the enhanced radiation concept, despite the continued reluctance of the Pentagon to supply crucial technical data. As a result of the explicit guidelines and access to information, the ACIS for the Lance ERW drafted by ACDA in June differed remarkably from the statements already submitted. The new statement used the term "enhanced radiation," which had been deleted in earlier unclassified versions, and explained that enhanced radiation "is achieved by fusion reactions that produce high energy

neutrons."[30] The arms control impact analysis concluded that "this weapon has no arms control advantages. To the extent it has any impact on ongoing arms control negotiations, the impact would be marginally negative."[31] The earlier ACIS on the enhanced radiation warhead for the 8-inch nuclear projectile had reached the opposite conclusion, that "this warhead . . . has been, and will continue to be, consistent with U.S. treaties, negotiations, and policies."[32]

The new statement provoked many objections when it was circulated for interagency review. Several officials close to the events commented that the ACIS on the Lance warhead was "inconsistent" with those for the nuclear artillery shells. DoD, ERDA, and the NSC scorned a procedure that required them to be critical of defense programs. At this time, the major objective of officials assigned to the neutron bomb case was the formation of a coherent policy to facilitate the production and deployment of ERWs. Those concerned with Alliance relations vigorously objected to a statement that would, in their view, add further strain to the already troubled transatlantic dialogue by taking a negative view of a weapon the United States had asked the allies to deploy on their territory. The interagency review on the Lance ACIS was described by one official as a "difficult, tortuous debating process among the various agencies and bureaucracies. A bit of scrambling around and much debate on terms occurred." Even ACDA officials saw the procedure as an "excruciating bureaucratic process," requiring interagency approval and recommendation whose purpose was, in many ways, diametrically opposed to the approving agencies' interests.

ACDA submitted its draft of the new Lance ACIS to the NSC on July 6. The contents were leaked to the press and the following day both European and American papers reported that, in a recent memo, ACDA had warned the White House that a decision to go ahead with full production of the neutron bomb and to install it on missiles and artillery might hurt SALT and compromise the administration's attempts to get new agreements on nonproliferation.[33] On the same day a White House press secretary informed the Senate that ACDA's warning on adverse implications for arms control negotiations was "flatly incorrect."[34] ACDA's statement raised concerns about the weapon's potentially negative impact on ongoing arms control negotiations. One week later, the Senate was still waiting for the analysis it had requested almost three weeks earlier. On the morning of July 13, several hours before the Senate was scheduled to resume debate on the neutron bomb, Senator Humphrey phoned Secretary of Defense Harold Brown with a "strong suggestion" that the ACIS be submitted to the Senate immediately. Realizing that congressional rejection of funds for the ERW would provoke an outcry from the defense community, Brown went immediately to the president. The Senate later reported that "the order was given to present . . . at once the impact statement, and that means that this statement is before us [the Senate]

before the NSC has had full time to analyze all of its significance."[35] Apparently, the NSC had not been able to reconcile the differences between the DoD and ACDA versions of this ACIS before it was sent to Congress.

The ACIS episode was a microcosm of the entire ERW controversy, characterized by competing interests and bureaucratic confusion. Different approaches to the ACIS process reflected the different interests of the federal bureaucracies. The Carter administration was characterized by a tolerance of diversity, repeatedly demonstrated by public disagreements between Secretary of State Cyrus Vance and the President's Advisor on National Security Zbigniew Brzezinski. But Carter would soon pay the price for not having a unified administration position. The public exposure of this squabble detracted from the administration's efforts to reach a consensus with the allies on ERWs. If agreement within the government was impossible, how could the Alliance be expected to reach a consensus? Carter soon became caught in a crossfire between critics and supporters, contributing to his adoption of a "wait and see" stance on the program.

The Senate Debate

The Senate debates on July 1 and 13 are notable for exposing the domestic political constraints that would influence the future course of events. Most senators had not been aware of the proposals before they became front-page news, in spite of a report published by the Armed Services Committee in May outlining in specific terms the fiscal year 1978 budget proposals for ERWs.[36] But even though most senators agreed they lacked sufficient information on the issues, in the approximately 12 hours of debate the Senate did cover the critical military and political issues concerning ERWs. Debate on the crucial military issues illustrates the ambiguity in U.S. and NATO policy for TNW use and why rationales for their deployment were so easily misconstrued. The crucial issue was one on which the proponents and critics began with agreement on a common understanding and then saw the consequences in precisely the opposite fashion. The fundamental military question was how ERWs would affect the balance of deterrence and defense in Central Europe: "Is deterrence better achieved if the other side thinks we are *more* likely to go to war but with *less* destructive weapons, or if it thinks we are *less* likely to go to war but with *more* destructive weapons?"[37] [Emphasis added.]

Both sides agreed that the reduction in collateral damage would make the use of enhanced radiation warheads more feasible in any eventual conflict. The proponents presented the same arguments as former Secretary of Defense Schlesinger had enunciated in 1975: A Warsaw Pact perception that NATO is more likely to use these weapons that reduce collateral damage increases the credibility of the deterrent against any Warsaw Pact incursion into NATO territory and therefore makes the actual probability of use less likely.

Proponents claim that the use of existing TNWs would cause so much damage to German cities and populace that NATO might never willingly order tactical nuclear strikes and thus would be effectively "self-deterred" from stopping a Warsaw Pact attack.[38] Opponents argued that if nuclear weapons are used first by NATO forces, no matter how small, their use will cause rapid escalation to full-scale nuclear war. Critics claimed that ERWs would "blur" the distinction between conventional and nuclear warfare by allowing NATO to think that TNWs could be employed without provoking the use of strategic nuclear weapons.[39] They believed that the threshold between nuclear and conventional warfare must be clearly demarcated and maintained sufficiently high to forestall all but "last resort" rationales for crossing it. The dilemma hinges on whether "tactical" or "limited" nuclear war can actually be controlled, either with present NATO targeting procedures or under any imaginable circumstances. Since the only answers to these questions are entirely matters of judgment and "faith" and since the questions all relate directly back to the verbal gymnastics of all tactical nuclear warfare doctrine, conclusions cannot be much more than dogmatic verbal formulations.

Several tangential military issues were also inconclusively deliberated by Congress. First, concern was expressed that unless the Soviet Union deployed TNWs with similar reduced collateral damage effects, little or nothing would be gained in terms of the total amount of destruction to property and populace in the battlefield areas. If the Warsaw Pact responded to conflict in which NATO had initiated use of ERWs on its territory with the higher-yield TNWs in the Soviet arsenal, then the "damage-limiting" advantage of ERWs would be immediately nullified. Second, the weapons' military effectiveness was questioned on the basis of contingency studies by the Pentagon indicating that the biological effects of neutron radiation might be delayed so that its victims would not be immediately incapacitated. Senator Heinz reported that the study found "that if victims of incapacitating agents became so sick that they retain little faith in living but still linger on for days, they may fight all the more tenaciously, suffering to die heroically by the bullet."[40] Third, doubts were raised about the weapons' ability to spare allied civilians, since the enhanced radiation effects would still kill or injure anyone, troops or noncombatants alike, irradiated by an enhanced radiation detonation. A crisis situation might create chaotic conditions in which ERWs would be detonated too close to the ground, thereby increasing the radius of enhanced radiation effects and possibly spilling over into civilian areas. The opponents' concern was exacerbated by what they incorrectly perceived as plans for NATO to order hundreds of enhanced radiation strikes if the Alliance were to stop Warsaw Pact armour from dispersing throughout NATO's rear areas following a successful penetration of NATO's defensive line.

An issue that provoked European as well as congressional opposition to the ERW proposal was the argument by Senate critics that "the bomb might

siphon off money that could be spent on a conventional defense of Europe which would accomplish the same objective."[41] Although this allegation was disputed by U.S. supporters, even allied proponents were unwilling to accept a trade-off between ERWs and conventional weapons. An adequate conventional posture is believed to be NATO's first and least destructive line of defense. Thus European governments would be alarmed by the assertion of some Senators that ERWs might "discourage . . . the Pentagon from putting money into conventional weapons."[42] Some senators were equally worried that "if we introduce a neutron bomb which our allies think we are more likely to employ if war should break out in Europe, what incentive do we give them to make a harder effort to supply additional conventional arms?"[43]

Another echo of European unease raised during the Senate debate concerned the humanitarian implications of ERWs. Opponents charged that neutron weapons represent a "literally dehumanizing" method of killing[44] and that therefore they are illegal under existing treaties and principles of international law. Senator Heinz was convinced that "death by neutron radiation smacks of the sort of chemical and biological warfare which had historically outraged civilized nations and which the US has at times strongly condemned."[45] Rather than killing or injuring by direct physical trauma, neutron radiation emitted by the warhead's detonation attacks the cellular processes of living things, causing death or injury over a period of time, as determined by the dosage received. Because studies by the Defense Department indicated that at intermediate ranges of exposure, death might not occur for weeks, one effect of an attack using ERWs could be a battlefield on which thousands of troops were so-called walking ghosts, that is, soldiers who had been exposed to a lethal intensity of radiation but were not yet physically incapacitated. Whether the suffering associated with such a battle would be any more "unnecessary" than a battlefield devastated by standard fission devices was one point of dispute in the debate over the legality of ERWs. Precisely because ERWs were designed to "optimize" the radiation effects of nuclear weapons, opponents considered them inhumane and illegal.

The weapons' supporters countered these contentions with two arguments. First, they noted that one of the cardinal objectives of U.S. arms control policy, and indeed one of the central tenets of the rules of war throughout history, is the concept of restricting the devastation of war to the battlefield, with damage to noncombatants minimized. To the degree that ERWs reduce collateral damage, proponents of these weapons maintained that their deployment would be consistent with these goals. Second, this point of view holds that the ultimate morality of ERWs rests in the lessened prospects for war that could be attributable to the greater deterrent effect of these weapons. Samuel T. Cohen, the so-called father of the neutron bomb, explained that "all military weapons, more correctly their employment, are immoral." Thus the humanitarian aspects of the enhanced radiation weapons "must be assessed in the context of a vastly different morality—the great obscenity of war itself." He added:

Most Americans feel that the greatest obscenity would be nuclear war. If fighting such a war would be humanly immoral to an extreme, then taking the necessary means to deter its outbreak can only be construed as a moral imperative. It is in this context that the development of any nuclear weapons must be judged. This includes the neutron bomb.[46]

Despite the hotly contested military and moral issues, the decisive factor in the Senate's vote was a procedural issue. All but the most ardent advocates of the weapons vigorously objected to approving funds for weapons to which the president was not yet committed. Carter did not become involved with the budget request for ERWs until the media brought it into the limelight, and he had then asked Congress to approve funds before he made his decision on whether to proceed with production. In a letter to the Senate of July 11, Carter indicated that he would not make his decision on production of the weapons until mid-August, after careful consideration of the ACIS and of a Pentagon study that had just been commissioned.[47] He made public his noncommittal stance in a press conference the following day with this statement: "I have not yet decided whether to approve the neutron bomb."[48] This unusual public announcement created doubts in the minds of many senators, not only about the military utility of the weapons (if it was clearly desirable and in the country's national interest, why would the president not offer his unqualified support?), but also, and perhaps more importantly, about the procedural role that the president seemed to be asking Congress to play.

The heart of the matter was as much the process of decision making as the decision itself. Senator Heinz made clear that the Senate was debating not just the weapons' contribution to allied or national security but that "we are also talking about the very way we are making our decision." He explained that "it is a good principle for the President to keep his options open on this. But by the same token, it is a pretty good principle for the Congress to keep its options open, too."[49] Opponents hoped, but also feared, that the president would decide not to order production of the weapons; the fear being that congressional authorization would be viewed as a "rubber stamp" of the president's decision rather than as a reasoned judgment by the legislature. Both proponents and critics demanded assurance that the Senate would not be publicly humiliated "if the President by August 15 decided he is not going to do this. We will have given him the money. We will have voted it, and they will have a lot of egg on their faces."[50] Thus the Senate's final vote on July 13 was not a reflection of the perceived military value of the weapon. The Senate approved the bill containing the funds, adding a minor qualification that, should the president decide to deploy the weapons, Congress would have 45 days in which to pass a resolution disapproving the action. The provision was in the form of an amendment, passed 74-19, cosponsored by the majority leader, Senator Byrd, and the minority leader, Senator Baker, prohibiting

production of ERWs until the president certified that production is in the national interest, and giving Congress the authority to disapprove production if both Houses of Congress passed a concurrent resolution to do so within 45 days of such presidential certification.[51] Opponents had preferred a one-House veto but when that amendment appeared certain to be defeated, they compromised a two-House veto.

The House debates in September struck similar procedural themes. Congressman Christopher Dodd felt that "the Congressional and Presidential decision making processes have been less than fully adequate in dealing with the neutron warhead production decision."[52] He also thought that Congress must have a "reasoned debate" on the ERW, as a result of insufficient and misleading information. He unsuccessfully attempted to table an amendment that "would allow Congress to fulfill its constitutional role as equal partner in deciding our Nation's national security policies."[53]

The Senate decisions to compromise and to demand that the president share the responsibility for the production decision parallels the decision-making process between the United States and its European allies on the neutron weapon. The legislature wanted the executive to bear an equal burden of the responsibility, and subsequent political accountability, for the production of ERWs. Similarly, the administration would soon adopt the position that "the responsibility for this deployment rests equally upon the NATO allies as a burden as well as upon us, the manufacturers of them."[54] Just as the Senate wanted the American public to hold the president equally accountable for the production of ERWs, the administration wanted the world to know that this action is being taken with "the approval of our NATO allies."[55] Washington feared that the public would construe an affirmative decision as America's preferred position without laying some of the responsibility on European governments. This perception was butressed not only by media coverage of the events implying that Carter was the sole decision maker but also by the uncertain attitude of the allies to the use of ERWs on their territory. Both the European press and the public were extremely critical of the weapons. But European governments had quietly supported this weapon in earlier consultations on TNW modernizaiton. Now that European publics were informed, their opinions altered their governments' position in private consultative forums. European governments were now publicly uncommitted, despite their private support. Senator Pell expressed the resentment some Senators felt at allied governments' neutrality:

> I am concerned here, because, as so often happens when Uncle Sam is made Uncle Sucker, the NATO governments are saying one thing to us privately—"Go ahead, fellows, we would like to move ahead with the new bomb,"—but then when you talk about public opinion in Europe and ask foreign friends how they feel about this weapon they seem to be opposed.[56]

Congressman Dodd asserted that Europe's position should be the decisive factor in Congress's decision: "European ambivalence is enough reason for Congress to refrain from approving production until more substantial discussions take place in NATO."[57]

In the past, unpublicized and unpoliticized decisions on nuclear weapons had usually been made unilaterally by the United States, with European acquiescence. The normal weapons acquisition process for American–produced, NATO-Europe-deployed arms involves at least two stages: production in the United States and deployment in Europe. Under ordinary circumstances Washington would reach a decision to produce a new weapon by congressional appropriation and presidential approval. NATO governments would have been briefed on U.S. intentions prior to the production decision so that any disagreement could be settled quietly before the American decision was made public. The contribution of NATO governments to the deployment decision is generally similar to ratification of American intentions, with European input primarily involving technical questions on where the weapon should be based. But in the case of ERWs, the issue had been exposed even before the administration had formulated a position on production, let alone consulted with European governments on deployment. With the world watching and listening, the scope of disagreement over the weapons, and hence the scope of the conflict, had widened. The United States would soon attempt to change the rules of the nuclear decision-making process: NATO nuclear decisions would now follow a pluralist model. The Senate debate anticipated the administration's move by asking the president to

> make certain that the various allies and others in the world know that this is not just American saber-rattling or a determination to forge ahead, but that such a step is done with the full approval of the NATO governments. They should also bear some of the responsibility for the deployment of the weapons because, if they were opposed, in fact, we know these weapons would not be deployed.
>
> So let not the bar of public opinion in the world only criticize the US if we do deploy these weapons. The onus should be shared equally by the European governments.[58]

WASHINGTON'S "HOT POTATO"

The way in which a president defines an issue usually establishes the general direction of the government's actions toward a specific goal. In weighing the pros and cons of an issue, the president will invariably consider both domestic political factors and foreign policy and national security considerations. While the president may be reluctant to admit that he is taking domestic political

interests into account, he knows that every issue, however marginal, is somehow related to his maintenance of effective power and perhaps to his reelection. As Morton Halperin has noted, "domestic political considerations and personal interests are an inescapable part of the decision process, especially at the White House."[59]

The exercise of presidential power is often an exercise in accommodating as many different interests as necessary to secure, in the short run, the adoption of a particular policy, and in the long run, the continuation of effective power. In order to do so, a president's behavior is often characterized by what Halperin calls "uncommitted thinking."[60] Exposed to many issues at once with many different pressures involved and habitually confronted with uncertainty and a variety of information channels, the president may adopt different patterns at different times for the same problem. He may respond at any one time to whichever pressures are momentarily strongest, whether they come from particular elements in the bureaucracy, from foreign governments, or from his own domestic political concerns. The decisive pressure is apt to be the one that, in the president's view at that moment, best fulfills his policy goals and assures his continued leadership.

Carter's dilemma in deciding what to do with the neutron bomb involved reconciling the various and often divergent pressures that converged upon him with the public exposure of the weapon. From the press he learned of the public's predominantly negative opinion and probably realized that any action he took would be widely covered by the media and subjected to public scrutiny. From Congress he had received qualified support for production and deployment of the weapon, but he had also been appraised, by the myriad of issues raised in the congressional debates, of the domestic political consequences of a decision either for or against the weapon. In light of the fact that the weapon had become a matter for public dispute before the administration had taken a stand on the issue, and Carter had then asked Congress to approve funds essentially to give him time to take a stand, he was now beholden to Congress to reciprocate the confidence they had reposed in him. The bureaucracies bombarded him with their own partial interests, derived from their stakes in the issue. Finally, he had to assess the pressure from the allies: whether or not they would support the weapon, and how European opposition to his position on the issue would affect his leadership both abroad and at home. All these pressures helped to shape the president's perspective on the neutron bomb.

The President's worldview contributed to his reluctance to take a stand on the issue. With so much adverse publicity on both sides of the Atlantic, any decision would exact a price on the president's foreign policies. If he decided to go ahead with production he would seem to be contradicting his already firm commitments to human rights and disarmament. How could he utter "freedom from oppression" and "kill people but preserve property" in one breath? In his

inaugural address, just six months earlier, he had spoken of dreaming of the day when nuclear weapons could be rid from the earth, saying that his "most cherished" hope was to contribute to progress in that direction. Neutron weapons would certainly not help him fulfill that vision. Yet if he chose instead to cancel production he would not only lose favor with the military but would also appear to be backing down under pressure from Moscow, which had already issued its usual condemnation of Western military improvements, calling the neutron bomb a "diabolical toy."[61] There was pressure from the diplomatic and defense bureaucracies to take positive action on defense in light of Carter's record to date on defense matters: He had cancelled the B-1 bomber without exacting a price from the Soviets and his "super" SALT proposal of spring 1977 had been rejected outright by Moscow. Most importantly, though, Carter, with a penchant for detail, felt he had not had time to fully consider his options. For Carter, the way the decision was made was as important as the decision itself. He had to convince himself that he was making the right decision, whatever it was.

In addition to weighing political concerns against personal convictions, Carter, the nuclear engineer, was faced with assessing the military implications of ERWs. This brought him to the heart of NATO's doctrinal dilemma and allowed him to find arguments both for and against the weapon's military value. He let the public know he could see both sides of the issue, though the press construed them according to its own convictions. In support, he contended that enhanced radiation weaponry could increase NATO's capability to deter a conventional or tactical nuclear attack by the Warsaw Pact and, if deterrence should fail, to minimize collateral damage: "TNWs, including those for battlefield use, have strongly contributed to deterrence of conflict in Europe. I believe we must retain the option they provide, and modernize it."[62] In particular, the president endeavored to allay fears that the availability of ERWs would make him more likely to order their use: "A decision to cross the nuclear threshold would be the most agonizing decision to be made by any President. I can assure you that these weapons would not make that decision any easier."[63] On the other hand, he acknowledged that once the nuclear threshold had been crossed, unacceptable damage might result: "My guess is that the first use of atomic weapons might very well lead to a rapid and uncontrolled escalation in the use of even more powerful weapons, with a possible worldwide holocaust resulting."[64] He conceded that despite the potential for lower collateral damage from NATO's use of ERWs, the employment of these weapons would be no less likely than the employment of current NATO TNWs to moderate Soviet retaliation with its larger TNWs.[65] Thus he acknowledged that unless the Soviets adopted comparable technology, their response with existing warheads could create the same kind of devastation that NATO's low-yield TNWs are designed to avoid. Moreover, Carter's spokesmen cautioned that if Soviet leaders perceive that the deployment of ERWs makes NATO's use of TNWs

even marginally more plausible, their incentive to preempt NATO's first use of TNWs would actually increase. In short, the principal political-military dilemma facing the president's decision on ERW production and deployment was to resolve whether the perceived gains for deterrence associated with these weapons outweighed the perceived risks of a lowered nuclear threshold.

These are tough questions, with no definitive answers, and Carter had his own personal doubts about the political utility of nuclear weapons. His background and idealistic personal convictions led him to try to minimize the role of force in diplomacy and international relations. Of course he realized that he could not immediately disarm the world. But he wanted that vision to be the cornerstone of his foreign policy. Controlling proliferation of nuclear weapons was a major component of his foreign policy program. In an interview shortly before his election, Carter had laid down three tenets of nuclear responsibility, including the need for "new international action to limit the spread of nuclear weapons." He linked this to U.S. weapons acquisition: "I believe we have little right to ask others to deny themselves such weapons for the indefinite future unless we demonstrate meaningful progress toward the goal of control, reduction and ultimately, elimination of nuclear arsenals."[66]

Arms control and disarmament were also high priorities on Carter's checklist of foreign policy objectives, but he had no clear or consistent idea about how to achieve them. But he did know what he did not want—a foreign policy similar to the Nixon-Ford era. Carter's campaign for the presidency had been largely a campaign against Kissinger's foreign policy. "As far as foreign policy goes," Carter had proclaimed during a televised debate with Gerald Ford in 1976, "Mr. Kissinger has been President of the country." Carter was determined to take a different stylistic approach to foreign policy. He came into office resolved that no one in his administration—neither Brzezinski nor Vance nor Brown—would monopolize influence or presidential thinking in the way that Henry Kissinger had managed to do with both Nixon and Ford. He was determined to make decisions on the basis of "cabinet government," a collegial consensus guided by his own ideas and instincts.[67] But his personal convictions often clashed with his political instincts on matters as weighty as nuclear decisions. Carter's proclivity to weigh every option carefully before deciding often made him appear indecisive. While he deliberated he became vulnerable to the personal views and political interests of his close advisors, who, early on, supported ERWs.

With allies and enemies, Congress and the administration, Carter wanted to establish a new approach to foreign policy. This novel approach was based on strong personal convictions and domestic political considerations. It was designed to reestablish the credibility of the presidency in the United States, and it became a decisive factor in shaping the president's perspective on how to handle the neutron bomb. In his attempt to eradicate the legacy of the Nixon–Kissinger era, fraught with Vietnam and Watergate, he had to dispel

feelings of "war-mongering" and dishonesty from the presidency. He would be a new type of leader, the people's voice, more liberal and open; he would give others a chance to air their views. Included in this view were the European allies. Though not well versed in the complexities of Alliance politics, Carter knew that the Europeans had often complained that the United States was trying to force their hand on nuclear matters; he knew, too, that Kissinger's attempt to uplift the U.S.-European spirit of cooperation in his 1973 "Year of Europe" had ended in disaster. Thus when confronted with Alliance problems early in his administration, he thought one way of inspiring a new mood of Alliance partnership might be to bring the allies into the decision making process. In Carter's opinion, a more pluralistic approach to allied decisions would not only positively distinguish his foreign policy from that of the previous administration but would also alleviate some of the burdens associated with nuclear decisions. The idea of building an Alliancewide consensus on the neutron bomb issue seemed to be an appealing way to avoid a major domestic row with Congress. Recall that the Senate had stipulated that action on ERWs be "taken with the approval of our NATO allies."[68] What better way to assure Congress that the allies approved of the weapon than to adopt a decision-making process whereby the allies would make public their commitment to deploy the weapon?

Many inside observers have noted that Carter was uncomfortable with the leadership role in the Alliance in that it required him to bear the responsibilities for nuclear decisions for all NATO countries. As reduction of America's reliance on nuclear power, both military and civilian, was one of Carter's major policy objectives, he was reluctant to deal with nuclear issues that would force him into an adversarial position with powerful domestic constituencies, particularly the military. Halperin has noted that a basic aim of all presidents is to avoid the appearance of failure.[69] Presidents are thus reluctant to undertake programs in the foreign policy field if they believe their initiatives have only a modest chance of succeeding. Carter did not have such a choice with the neutron bomb. The issue was thrust upon him and he was therefore forced to act. But he could try to lessen the burden of his responsibility. Halperin's insights are also applicable here: A president will proceed "warily on those issues that arouse major passions and interests either in the population as a whole or within a significant group whose support he values on other issues, domestic or foreign."[70] Carter's reluctance to shoulder the burden of NATO's nuclear responsibilities bolstered his view that the Europeans deserved to bear a greater portion of the burden for their defense.

But with all his good intentions, Carter did not understand European politics and the sensitivity of the Europeans to nuclear matters. Carter's handling of the ERW issue reflects his muddled perception of the allies' own domestic political constraints. He interpreted European complaints about lack of consultation on nuclear matters as a desire to have a greater voice in

weapons acquisitions for NATO. But these complaints were really a veiled attempt to procure a stronger American commitment to a form of deterrence that would assure Europe's security by the American strategic nuclear umbrella. Carter's misperception of European constraints seem powerfully to have reinforced his assessment of his own domestic political constraints: that building a consensus within NATO on the neutron bomb was the most likely way to assure its domestic support, both in the United States and Europe. But despite their rhetoric, Europeans do *not* want the responsibility of making nuclear decisions. European publics and parliaments impose stringent constraints on foreign policy, which is closely linked to cultural and economic notions of détente. As the first country to possess nuclear weapons, the United States has a history of nuclear decisions, making leadership in the Alliance on nuclear matters a natural role. Europe, more likely to be the target of a nuclear attack than either the United States or the USSR, and lacking a familiarity with nuclear decisions (with the exception of Britain and France), has always been reluctant to arm itself with weapons that will destroy what it seeks to preserve. "Shorter-range weapons have always been a sensitive issue for the Europeans," one observer remarked; "the U.S. doesn't always take into account the luxury it enjoys in being a great distance from the immediate threat."

The lack of sensitivity to European concerns cannot be blamed on Carter alone. The new administration had very few high-level foreign policy officials with good contacts in and strong sympathies for Europe. In a sense, with the accession of the Carter administration, the American foreign policy establishment had undergone a generational change. The group of American professionals and foreign service officers who were experienced in NATO affairs were, for the most part, people who grew up during World War II and were familiar with the birth of NATO. Many of them were European descendents and had a personal interests in U.S.-European relations. Like Kissinger, their service culminated and terminated with the Nixon and Ford administrations.

Beginning with the Vietnam era, however, a new, younger generation or type of policymaker emerged whose focus was directed more toward Asia, the Middle East, and the Third World, in general. These were relatively new areas of major international tension. The dimensions of their problems were considerably different from those of Europe and required new and varied forms of analysis. The Carter administration was particularly sensitive to this "new agenda" in the world politics, which included human rights, nonproliferation, and the North-South dialogue. Problems of European security tended to be minimized by the new generation; the problems they perceived as important were primarily economic and cultural.[71] As Europe's economic strength grew, these officials were inclined to associate yearnings for European economic leadership with political leadership within the Alliance. They tended to

interpret the revival of interest in European defense as the result of the decline of tension in other spheres, like Asia, more than as a reflection of Europe's growing concern over the credibility of America's commitment to European security.

This attitude was not conducive to good relations with Europe, especially West Germany. Some observers even detected an anti-German bias in the new administration.[72] Carter's National Security Council, chaired by Zbigniew Brzezinski, was particularly bent on erasing the tarnished reputation that body had earned during the Nixon-Ford era. In putting on a new face, the NSC felt it had to destroy all the "Nixon-Ford elements," of which a crucial one was the Bonn-Washington axis. Under Kissinger, relations between Washington and Bonn had flourished, and Kissinger and Schmidt had developed a close friendship. Those concerned with European affairs in the Carter administration were wary of the Bonn-Washington axis, which they associated with Kissinger's legacy. Moreover, they felt that the Germans were generally too conservative, too security conscious. In their view, European politics should be less concerned with German military matters and more concerned with improving relations with the French.[73]

Thus when neutron weapons became an issue in Alliance politics, German-American relations were already at a low point. In the State Department, a rumor was circulated that Pincus had gotten his story from someone who deliberately wanted to irritate the Germans. Problems in SALT only exacerbated existing tensions. While controversy over the neutron bomb was but a thorn in the thicket of SALT negotiations, SALT had a lasting impact on the decision-making process for ERWs. The policy planners and diplomats who were responsible for the ongoing SALT talks in all its multifarious facets were also the individuals who were charged with handling the ERW controversy. Their greater interest in SALT dictated their determination to seek an outcome on ERW that would be favorable to SALT. SALT dwarfed ERW in importance to these men, but for precisely that reason the molehill that was ERW eventually became a mountain, and volcanic one at that. One participant later commented that

> a major part of the policy problem in the U.S. seemed to be its relative subordination to the ongoing SALT talks. Because the same policy planners and diplomats were running SALT and ERW, the priority of SALT goals took precedence to ERW outcomes. High-ranking officials in State, DoD, and the NSC didn't turn their attention to ERW until it was almost too late to achieve a positive outcome without damaging alliance relations. ERW consultations ran parallel to SALT negotiations but the former was in last place before the race began.

Shortly after neutron weapons became the subject of heated public debate, an interagency task force comprised of officials from the NSC, DoD, and State

Department was set up to "work the issue." Although they knew something had to be done, they as yet had no directive from the president. Carter did not address the issue in public until July 12, more than a month after Pincus's article first appeared and one day before the final Senate debate on production funds, at which time he announced: "I have not yet decided whether to approve the neutron bomb. I do think it ought to be one of our options, however."[74] The initial question for State Department officials assigned to the task force was how to proceed with the allies without clear directions from the president. They had to consult directly with their European counterparts, and a remark by Georg Leber, the West German defense minister, that he had not been previously informed of the ERW proposal, presented State Department officials with a formidable diplomatic task. To these officials the president had two choices: either adopt a multilateral approach to the decision by asking the allies for their views or attempt to move the issue unilaterally by dictating a decision. Given the bad publicity in which the substantive issues were shrouded, the second option was quickly ruled out as involving too great a political risk for the new administration. Despite the precarious domestic political situation, the State Department could not avoid consultations with the allies, even if they lacked substantive direction. American negotiators were reluctant to take on this task: "The eruption of a media-fueled political volcano left a crater in alliance relations which had to be filled with consultative procedures, however vacuous," quipped a State Department participant.

So without a presidential directive, the State Department set to work, trying to heal the wounds in Europe. When the Europeans asked whether the president wanted to deploy the weapons, the State Department admitted that no decision had as yet been made. The American negotiators thought the proper course of action was to apologize to the allies for the adverse publicity, admit that the neutron bomb had become a political snag in Alliance relations, and act in concert, primarily to preclude the Soviet Union from taking advantage of the disparate situation by forcing or coercing Europe into a position in which no amount of American persuasion would convince Europe to accept U.S. policy. During summer 1977, in private consultations, the State Department tried to move the allies toward an agreement on a joint decision for production and deployment. Bilateral negotiations were held with Britain and West Germany and consultations were formally carried out in NATO forums, all without result. The State Department was hoping to coax a positive opinion from the two crucial allies, Bonn and London, in order to substantiate the controversial issue for the president and get him to decide in favor of its course of action. The Americans emphasized the potential contribution of ERWs to NATO's defense posture and downplayed any doubts they had about the weapon's military effectiveness. But the extent of the political venture the Europeans felt they were being prevailed upon to join was not fully understood or personally embraced by any diplomat or policymaker in the summer

months. The American negotiators thought of the ERW simply as a "follow-on warhead for existing nuclear artillery," a modest military capability with only minor political significance.

They misread the weapon's impact on the European domestic political scene. The Europeans wanted greater acknowledgment of its political importance and a firm commitment that the United States, in fact, believed in the weapon's value for deterrence and defense. A great show of leadership was required from the United States, but the various bureaucracies involved never agreed on the weapon's value. If all the agencies and departments concerned could have rallied around certain arguments advanced by the president in favor of deployment, such as reduced collateral damage, the Europeans would have felt more comfortable joining a decision. But Carter had not yet set a course of action that could unite the administration's efforts to persuade the allies to deploy ERWs. Instead, a whole series of inter- and intragency panics followed during that summer, characterized by a salient lack of direction from the NSC and White House staffs who were supposedly coordinating the effort.

In retrospect, a State Department official conceded that it was impossible for the United States to approach the allies undecided and expect them to be able to take a decision. Despite European criticism time and time again of America's unilateral approach to Alliance decision making, European heads of state knew that the sensitive nature of nuclear decisions struck at the core of European society and its external relations. But in these early months, Carter and his staff hesitated and vacillated, fearful of taking a course of action that would give the impression either of increasing European security over the perceived objections of the Europeans or of compromising European security through the success of Soviet propaganda. The U.S. objective was to avoid a politically vulnerable situation. The majority of American policymakers concluded that the only feasible solution was withholding a commitment on production until allied leaders offered concrete assurances that they would permit deployment.

NOTES

1. Richard Neustadt, *Alliance Politics* (New York: Columbia University Press, 1970), p. 61.

2. Interview with Walter Pincus, Washington *Post*, August 15, 1980.

3. Barry Rubin, "The Media and the Neutron Bomb," Washington *Review*, July 1978, p. 90.

4. Walter Pincus, Washington *Post*, June 6, 1977, p. 1.

5. Ibid.

6. Rubin, p. 90.

7. Alex A. Vardamis, "The Neutron Warhead: Stormy Past, Uncertain Future," *Parameters, Journal of the US Army War College* 8 (March 1978): 41.

8. Bernard Weinraub, "What Role for the Neutron Bomb?" New York *Times*, July 17, 1977, p. E4.

9. Rubin, p. 91.

10. Interview with Walter Pincus, August 15, 1980.

11. Alton Frye, "The High Risks of Neutron Weapons," Washington *Review*, July 17, 1977, p. B1.

12. Rubin, p. 93.

13. "No Neutron Warheads," Washington *Post*, June 26, 1977.

14. Walter Pincus, Washington *Post*, June 25, 1977.

15. U.S. Congress, House, 95th Cong., 1st sess., *Congressional Record*, June 14, 1977, H5835-79.

16. Washington *Post*, June 23, 1977, p. A1, and June 24, 1977, p. A25.

17. *US News and World Report*, July 25, 1977, p. 25.

18. U.S. Congress, Senate, 95th Cong., 1st sess., *Congressional Record*, July 1, 1977, S11427.

19. Ibid.

20. U.S. Congress, Senate, 95th Cong., 1st sess., *Congressional Record*, June 24, 1977, p. 10639 and July 13, 1977, p. S11748.

21. Duncan L. Clarke, *The Politics of Arms Control: The Role and Effectiveness of the U.S. Arms Control and Disarmament Agency* (New York: The Free Press, 1979), p. 191.

22. Ibid, p. 193.

23. Ibid, p. 205.

24. Milton Leitenberg, "Background Information on Tactical Nuclear Weapons (primarily in the European context)," *Tactical Nuclear Weapons: European Perspectives* (London: Taylor and Francis for the Stockholm International Peace Research Institute, 1978), p. 59.

25. The guidelines accompanying the 1975 authorizing legislation were extremely vague and provided no standards by which to assess the arms control impact of various weapons systems. Interviews with officials of the Arms Control and Disarmament Agency, Washington, D.C., August 21, 1980.

26. Ibid.

27. U.S. Congress, *Analysis of Arms Control Impact Statement Submitted in Connection with the Fiscal Year 1978 Budget Request*, 95th Cong., 1st sess., Congressional Research Service, Joint Committee Print, 1977, p. 368.

28. Ibid, pp. 153-68.

29. Clarke, p. 191.

30. U.S. Congress, House, *Additional Arms Control Impact Statements and Evaluations for Fiscal Year 1978*, Committee on International Relations, 95th Cong., 1st sess., December 1, 1977, p. 1.

31. Ibid, p. 3.

32. *Analysis of Arms Control Impact Statement*, p. 165.

33. *Financial Times* (London), July 7, 1977; *Daily Telegraph* (London), July 7, 1977.

34. U.S. Congress, Senate, 95th Cong., 1st sess., *Congressional Record* July 13, 1977, S11741.

35. Ibid.

36. U.S. Congress, Senate, Report of the Committee on Armed Services, *Energy Research and Development Administration Authorization—Military Applications, FY77 and FY78*, May 16, 1977, p. 13.

37. U.S. Congress, Senate, Senator Heinz, *Congressional Record*, July 1, 1977, S11428.

38. U.S. Congress, Senate, Senator Nunn, 95th Cong., 1st sess., *Congressional Record*, July 1, 1977, S11431.

39. U.S. Congress, Senate, Senator Hatfield, 95th Cong., 1st sess., *Congressional Record*, July 1, 1977, S11439.

40. *Congressional Record*, July 13, 1977, S11753.

41. U.S. Congress, Senate, Senator Heinz, *Congressional Record*, July 13, 1977, S11752.

42. U.S. Congress, Senate, Senator Heinz, *Congressional Record*, July 1, 1977, S11429.

43. U.S. Congress, Senate, Senator Church, *Congressional Record*, July 13, 1977, S11772.

44. Senator Heinz, July 1, 1977, S11429.

45. Ibid.

46. Quoted in Bernard Weinraub, "What Role for the Neutron Bomb?" New York *Times*, July 17, 1977, p. E4.

47. *Congressional Record*, July 13, 1977, S11757.

48. New York *Times*, July 13, 1977, p. A10.

49. *Congressional Record*, July 13, 1977, S11752.

50. U.S. Congress, Senate, Senator Javits, *Congressional Record*, July 13, 1977, S11777.

51. *Congressional Record*, July 13, 1977, S11789.

52. *Congressional Record*, September 13, 1977, H9312.

53. Ibid.

54. U.S. Congress, Senate, Senator Pell, *Congressional Record*, July 13, 1977, S11776.

55. Ibid.

56. Ibid, S11747.

57. U.S. Congress, House, *Congressional Record*, September 13, 1977, H9314.

58. Senator Pell, July 13, 1977, S11776.

59. Morton H. Halperin, *Bureaucratic Politics and Foreign Policy* (Washington, D.C.: The Brookings Institution, 1974), p. 63.

60. Ibid., p. 24.

61. "Russia Blasts U.S. on Neutron Bomb Plans," *International Herald Tribune*, August 1, 1977.

62. U.S. Congress, Senate, *Congressional Record*, July 13, 1977, S11755.

63. U.S. Congress, Senate, Letter by President Carter to Senator Stennis, 95th Cong., 1st sess., *Congressional Record*, July 13, 1977, S11748.

64. Ibid.

65. Richard P. Cronin and Robert G. Bell, "ERWs: The Neutron Bomb," Archived Issue Brief, IB 78085, Congressional Research Service, Library of Congress, October 19, 1978.

66. Jimmy Carter, "Three Steps Toward Nuclear Responsibility," *The Bulletin of Atomic Scientists* 32 October (1976): 10-11.

67. Strobe Talbott, *Endgame: The Inside Story of SALT II* (New York: Harper and Row, 1979), p. 41.

68. U.S. Congress, Senate, Senator Pell, *Congressional Record*, July 7, 1977, S11776.

69. Halperin, p. 72.

70. Ibid., p. 73.

71. Interview with Richard Burt, National Security Correspondent for the New York *Times*, Washington, D.C., August 20, 1980.

72. Ibid.

73. Ibid.

74. New York *Times*, July 13, 1977, p. A.10.

4

The West German Debate

The debate over ERWs in Europe was qualitatively different from the debate in the United States. Whereas much of the early American debate focused on who should make the first commitment, the legislature or the president, and when that commitment should be made, the European debate focused much more directly on the neutron bomb's overall implications for NATO TNW doctrine. The controversy created by the neutron bomb was far more intense in West Germany than in any other NATO country for the simple geopolitical reason that these weapons would be deployed on West German territory, NATO's first line of defense.

The European debate in summer 1977 focused almost entirely on the theoretical aspects of tactical nuclear war and the doctrinal ramifications of deploying ERWs in Europe. This debate reconfirmed the stark contrast between American and European interests in TNWs in general, and ERWs in particular, which can be traced to divergent conceptions of deterrence and defense. European government officials, informed observers, and the media gave little consideration to the decision-making aspects of the problem: It was assumed by all Europeans that Carter would eventually make a decision on whether to produce the weapons and only then would the issue of deployment be deliberated in bilateral channels and multilateral alliance forums. During summer 1977, West German Chancellor Schmidt did not anticipate the central role he would play in the resolution of the crisis. At that time he considered the weapon an American problem.

The quality and scope of the European debate is best examined from the German perspective, which included many elements of comparable concern to

other Europeans. Moreover, since the West German government would eventually be asked by the United States to take the lead in a European decision to deploy ERWs, the German debate is the most vital to this analysis.

The German chancellor, like the American president, was influenced by domestic political concerns as well as by national security interests. The sensitivity of nuclear issues in West Germany placed severe political constraints upon Chancellor Schmidt. Moreover, the strong opposition of powerful factions of the governing coalition severely restricted the government's ability to adopt a firm position on ERWs. The confusing signals from the United States, emanating from both the press and the administration, only compounded Schmidt's dilemma on how to handle the neutron bomb issue.

THE REACTION OF THE WEST GERMAN PRESS AND OF POLITICAL LEADERS

The West German public debate is best characterized by an observation made by Helmut Schmidt in 1962 when he complained of "the widespread tendency in the Federal Republic to judge military matters from an emotional standpoint and to shy away from penetrating, complex, and rational consideration of the situation."[1] Walter Pincus's article "Neutron Killer Warhead Buried in ERDA Budget"[2] and the subsequent American debate were widely covered in the West German press. Conservative papers such as *Die Welt* and *Die Frankfurter Allgemeine Zeitung*, and their defense commentators, supported the deployment of ERWs on German territory. The neutron bomb conforms with "the intellectual foundations of the strategy of 'flexible response,'" wrote *Die Welt*, and thus "strengthens the deterrent force."[3] *Frankfurter Allgemeine* praised the ERW as the first viable warfighting capability for NATO, a new departure from the deterrence-only conception of nuclear weapons deployed in Europe:

> The neutron projectile will change the battlefield. . . . New principles of fighting will have to be evolved and the present concept of deterrence will have to be revised, politically and strategically. All this will take time, and the public in America and Europe will have to get used to the idea that there are nuclear weapons which are not exclusively political weapons. . . .[4]

Conservative papers claimed that "none of the European allies would protest if the Americans began equipping their European-based tactical weapons with neutron warheads in the next year or two."[5] Left-wing and communist papers, such as *Die Wahrheit*, assailed the neutron bomb as an "extreme example of military madness,"[6] claiming that death "in a nuclear war would probably be even more cruel with the neutron bomb."[7] Like the reaction in the United States, the West German press exploited information on the technical features

of the warheads to convey the notion that ERWs primarily kill people and preserve buildings—the "supercapitalist" weapons. Those who did not read the political comments gathered this notion from looking at the profusion of cartoons in the press. Logically, the press paid close attention to the weapon's implications for issues relevant to West Germany, in particular the possible adverse effects of the weapon on arms limitation negotiations. Even some who felt that the weapon would enhance deterrence, like the *Sueddeutsche Zeitung*, added in the same sentence, "but it reduces the chances for a SALT agreement."[8] The *Rhein Zeitung* thought it "possible that Carter is playing a 'poker game' for a good starting position in the next round of SALT talks."[9] Other papers voiced concern about adverse effects on the trilateral test ban talks in Geneva.[10]

While such speculation was probably valid, many papers incorrectly surmised from Carter's urging Congress on July 12 to approve initial production funds that he had already commited himself to producing the weapons. *Die Welt's* Washington correspondent reported that "observers consider it unlikely that the report on the neutron bomb which the President has requested is likely to cause him to revise his present stand. Having more or less committed himself [on production and deployment of the bomb], he will be unable to shift his position."[11] With a view toward SALT, another paper interpreted Carter's alleged commitment as a bargaining tactic:

> Carter's newest spectacular announcement of the production of the disputed neutron bomb stresses his erratic and reciprocal willingness to achieve by hook or crook the goals he has set. Using this club, the U.S. President apparently wants to force the Soviets to the negotiating table. . . .[12]

Those who detected this intention in the ERW proposal generally condemned it: "Jimmy Carter, the President with the campaign promises to outlaw all nuclear weapons, has, with many of his arms decisions, increased rather than decreased the competition between the superpowers."[13] *Der Spiegel* accurately summarized the feeling in Europe: "Armament technicians have again developed a weapon which may appeal to nuclear war planners and NATO artillery men but which presents politicians with problems comparable to those of squaring the circle."[14]

The West German government refused to comment for several weeks. In the interim a prominent political figure provoked a national debate that contributed significantly not only to public opposition but also to the government's position on ERWs. The controversy was precipitated by Egon Bahr, executive secretary of the ruling SPD (Social Democratic Party) and intellectual architect of détente under former Chancellor Willy Brandt. Bahr, generally considered to be a man of cold intelligence and sober analysis,[15] denounced the neutron bomb as a "symbol of mental perversity" in an article

published in the SPD weekly *Vorwärts* under the headline "Is Mankind Going Crazy?"[16] Bahr's opening salvo was unexpected by government leaders and defense department officials who had hoped to push through the modernization program without much public attention.[17] Bahr's criticism that ERWs reverse normal values by killing humans but not destroying property, constituting a "mutation of human thinking," precipitated a political controversy in which the Conservatives focused more on rebutting Bahr than on debating the substantive issues.[18]

What motivated Bahr's moral attack on these weapons while the government and his party remained silent? Although Bahr seemed concerned that the deployment of ERWs would lower the nuclear threshold and make the possibility of war more likely, he may also have been motivated by domestic political factors unrelated to the weapons. First, he was troubled by the negative reaction in Eastern Europe to the ideological offensive of the Carter administration, which he perceived as stressing human rights at the expense of détente and arms limitation. Second, with his comment, Bahr, who had just been applauded by the SPD's conservative faction for ousting the chairman of the party's youth organization, suddenly won the favor of the party's left wing as well.

That the German public debate was organized around emotional and political lines was brought out by Theo Sommer, editor of *Die Zeit*, who noted in his weekly that public discussion had been characterized by an excess of emotion and "simple ignorance." The emotionally charged issue concerned not only the political and military implications of ERWs but also the entire range of TNWs in Europe: "Are we drifting once more, after an interval of 20 years, into another emotionally charged debate on the questions of defense and deterrence—again triggered off by the role of tactical atomic weapons in Central Europe?"[19] Sommer called for a "sober appraisal . . . of the technical and functional capability of the weapons themselves, the effect they are likely to have on the policy of deterrence, and finally, possible diplomatic consequences."[20] Examining the East-West military balance, he justified the deployment of neutron warheads as "a psychological answer to the Soviet's SS-X-20"[21] an intermediate–range ballistic missile (IRBM), about which concern was rapidly increasing in the West, but which was not included in the SALT negotiations. Although Sommer considered the possibility that ERWs might be used as a "bargaining chip" in East-West arms control negotiations, the more likely result would be to "speed up the tempo of the arms race . . . the faltering steps made in past years towards arms control would be wiped out. It is here that the fundamental objections to the neutron weapons lie, and not at the moral level on which Egon Bahr has sought to conduct the debate."[22] Sommer was most troubled by the ramifications for Alliance relations caused by the process through which the weapons had become the subject of debate:

The political aspects of the problem within NATO have to be considered. Up to now the responsible authorities in the European countries only know what they have read in the American press (a fact, incidentally, which is not a very shining testimonial to the openness of the Carter Administration).[23]

In the final analysis, Sommer predicted that the neutron bomb would not only aggravate East-West tension but would also put unnecessary strain on Alliance relations.

In the face of domestic uproar, the Bonn government tried to remain neutral. While youth organizations of both parties campaigned against deployment of the weapon, Chancellor Schmidt commented that it was "too early for the federal government to take a stand" because the United States had not yet made a decision on production.[24] He acknowledged that such weapons would pose "considerable psychological and strategic problems" for NATO, but intended to reserve final judgment until Carter informed him of his decision. He expected allied consultations to commence once the United States decided to seek deployment of the new weapons in West Germany. Defense Minister Georg Leber denied reports from NATO that German military officials were eager to add ERWs to NATO's nuclear arsenal: "It is not true that we Germans have shown special interest within NATO for the neutron bomb."[25] The Bundeswehr, however, had taken "a positive attitude to the subject."[26]

Schmidt's neutrality was based on his interpretation of the warhead's potential consequences for his national policy objectives, not on a particular aversion to ERWs or their doctrinal implications. He had at least three reasons for remaining publicly neutral, although his government had previously expressed its support for the weapons in private bilateral and NATO forums. First, he did not want to become the object of the public wrath that had been engendered by the neutron bomb. By early August the issue had erupted into a major domestic controversy, accurately described by an American observer: "The mounting dispute over the neutron bomb in the United States is likely to become a teacup-sized tempest compared to the storm over the issue now brewing in West Germany."[27]

Second, he may have hoped to reduce tension in German-American relations by staying out of the public discussion. He was "obviously trying not to aggravate relations between Bonn and Washington which have become increasingly strained since Carter's inauguration."[28] Schmidt had never held Carter in high esteem and the neutron bomb was certainly not going to be an issue that would improve either their personal rapport or bilateral relations. The German debate was beginning to aggravate anti-American sentiments in the Federal Republic. Foreign Minister Hans-Dietrich Genscher warned that "any discussion about the neutron bomb should avoid assuming an anti-American accent."[29] Even German supporters of ERW deployment were

critical of the way the decision was being handled in Washington, charging that the "United States is responsible for undermining NATO's self-assurance."[30] A common criticism, which would intensify as the debate dragged on, was that the United States was trying to preserve its security at the expense of Europe: "The United States is for the first time in a vulnerable position liable to nuclear attack, so Washington is trying to delegate the risk to others."[31] Third, and most important, Schmidt believed that no position was required of his government at the time. The first decision, regarding production, was an American responsibility; if Carter did not first make a commitment to produce the neutron bomb, Schmidt would never be able to convince the German people that its deployment would enhance German security.

REACTIONS OF WEST GERMAN PARTIES
TO THE NEUTRON BOMB

The views of the West German political parties decisively influenced the position of the Schmidt government on the neutron bomb. Like the congressional debates in the United States, the reactions of the political parties delineated the domestic political concerns that would constrain Schmidt's range of action. But German political parties, unlike their American counterparts, are constitutionally endowed with extensive authority to delimit the government's policies and actions. If the German government loses the support of its party or parties, the government can be disbanded. Thus political parties are the bulwark of the Federal Republic. Unlike the United States, "all political decisions in the Federal Republic are made by the parties and their representatives. There are no political decisions of importance in the German democracy which have not been brought to the parties, prepared by them, and finally taken by them."[32]

Opposition Parties: CDU/CSU (Christian Democratic Union/Christian Social Union)

In general, the conservative opposition supported the deployment of ERWs; however, given the dissension within the ruling SPD, this position did not give Schmidt license to support deployment.

Manfred Wörner, chaiman of the Defense Committee in the Bundestag and shadow defense minister of the conservative opposition, led the coalition in support of the deployment of ERWs. He was a powerful personality in German politics and his opinion on defense matters was highly regarded, even by the SPD. At the time, Conservatives held a plurality of the seats in the Bundestag. In an article published in English in fall 1977, Wörner examined NATO's doctrinal dilemma regarding TNWs and made a cogent case for their political value in Europe. Recapping the German paradox, he noted:

There is the belief, on the one hand, that TNWs contribute to the securing of the peace—but the fear, on the other hand, that a future conflict in Europe would mean inexorably the nuclear extinction of the Federal Republic of Germany and many other important parts of Europe. TNWs are central to the general numbing effect that the sheer magnitude of the problems of nuclear deterrence and defense in the European context has exerted on public opinion.[33]

Finding NATO's conventional posture inadequate to counter a massive conventional attack from the East, Wörner exhorted NATO to "exploit optimally all technological possibilities," to "assure that the conceptual, institutional and material preconditions are created for a possible use of TNWs," and to stress the possibility that any conflict may extend to the use of United States strategic nuclear systems.[34] Wörner emphasized the need for smaller and more mobile nuclear systems "that can minimize unintended casualties and damage to civilian populations and the civilian economy: ERWs, or so-called neutron bombs, clearly fall into this category."[35]

Few conservatives spoke out against deployment of ERWs; the comments of those who did were clearly overshadowed by Wörner's numerous approbations.[36]

The Free Democratic Party (FDP)

The FDP, the minority party in the governing coalition, was divided over the deployment of the neutron bomb on West German territory. Although Hans-Dietrich Genscher, vice-chancellor and foreign minister, and Jugar Mollemann, FDP defense spokesman, supported deployment, many local committees and the party's youth organization, the *Jungedemokraten*, opposed the weapons.[37] Given this split, the FDP did not make this issue a major problem within the social-liberal governing coalition. But the FDP's 39 seats in the Bundestag were crucial to the governing coalition's mandate. Schmidt had been reelected the previous December by only a one-vote majority. The opposition CDU/CSU, with 243 seats against the SPD's 214, had emerged as the strongest party in the Bundestag, and the governing coalition now had a majority of only ten seats.[38] One German political scientist has noted that "the FDP has held the balance of power in the Bundestag following most federal elections."[39] Thus the SPD's position hinged on the acquiescence of its governing partner, at a minimum.

The Social Democratic Party (SPD)

Schmidt's public neutrality on the neutron bomb reflected his inability to reconcile the dissension within his party. Although he personally supported

deployment, a number of leading party figures and the rank and file vehemently opposed the weapon.[40] Egon Bahr's emotional outburst was the most widely publicized. Hans Koschnick, the mayor of Bremen, deputy chairman of the SPD and chairman of the party's national security policy committee, argued that deployment of ERWs would lower the nuclear threshold and thus make deterrence less credible.[41] Koschnick also claimed that the use of neutron warheads on the central European battlefield would automatically provoke a more destructive retaliation by the Soviet Union, and that thereby not only the Federal Republic but the whole of Germany would be devastated by nuclear weapons.[42] Alfons Pawelczyk, chairman of the arms control subcommittee of the Bundestag, assailed the weapon's potential political liabilities for the ongoing arms control negotiations in Geneva and Vienna and for the delicate climate of détente between East and West Europe.[43] Unsurprisingly, the left-wing faction of the SPD, led by the Young Socialists, who had persistently demanded Bonn's withdrawal from NATO, deplored the weapons proposal.[44] Capitalizing on the relative inactivity of the older, more moderate rank and file, the *Jungsozialisten* were becoming increasingly active and influential in party politics at the local level, espousing foreign policy positions of unilateral disarmament and strict neutrality.[45] Helmut Schmidt, who belonged to the rightwing of the party, had attacked the Young Socialists in very harsh tones on several occasions,[46] in particular on their utopian approach to foreign policy.

Schmidt's potential supporters in the SPD offered the chancellor little positive reinforcement of his personal view of the weapon, probably because they, too, felt constrained by their party's predominantly negative reaction. Most Social Democrats who did not publicly oppose the weapon offered only evasive comments. Although Conrad Ahlers, a member of the Bundestag Defense Committee, had recited the military advantages of ERWs in the Bundestag debate, he refrained from actively endorsing deployment: "In my opionion, we will have to learn to live with the neutron bomb and include it in our defense concept."[47] Defense Minister Georg Leber was also careful not to commit himself and cautioned that further discussions are needed and that such decisions can only be made by NATO as a whole, not the Bonn government alone.[48]

Overall, a considerable portion of the SPD was opposed to the neutron bomb, mostly on humanitarian and military grounds, which are continually a matter of personal judgment and speculation. But the reluctance of Schmidt to support deployment in the initial phase of the transatlantic debate was motivated to a large extent by domestic political considerations, rather than by any inherent opposition to the weapons themselves. With only a slim majority in Parliament, the government could not afford to lose a vote in the Bundestag. As the German electorate was extremely sensitive to issues of nuclear policy, Schmidt had to take public opinion into account. With four state elections

scheduled for early 1978, the results of which would determine the majority in the upper chamber (the Bundesrat), the government could not ignore the views of supporters who had shifted their allegiance to the governing coalition for its laudable efforts toward détente, which could only be adversely affected by a weapon whose deployment was not receiving unanimous support in the West. The domestic political constraints on Schmidt dictated that while he need not reject the weapon outright, neither could he openly support it without being able to claim that Washington and other NATO countries were also responsible for the decision.

Schmidt's reticence was also prompted by his personal opinion of the American president. While the two men were equally self-assertive they were otherwise different in temperament and outlook. Schmidt, the calculating pragmatist, was baffled and at times annoyed by Carter, the moralizing idealist. The president complained that the chancellor was obstinate and didactic; the chancellor found the president erratic and inexperienced. Both tried to overcome their differences, but they never quite succeeded. They had already clashed on many major issues confronting the two countries. Schmidt had been irritated by Carter's request in March 1977 that the German government cancel its proposed sale of advanced nuclear equipment to Brazil. Schmidt greatly resented Carter's human rights policy, which the chancellor feared might endanger the further progress of détente and halt the westward migration of thousands of Germans still under communist rule. To the German chancellor, Carter's outspoken position on human rights was another example of the president's naive, amateurish, and zigzagging approach to foreign policy. The rapport of the two leaders was equally poor on NATO matters. Disagreement between Bonn and Washington flared over the issue of standardization of conventional weaponry deployed with the national armies of NATO member countries. Schmidt interpreted America's approach to standardization as a one-way flow of U.S. arms sales to Europe, adding strain to their already troubled economies.[49] The neutron warhead was another U.S. item that would eat into Europe's defense budgets. For all these reasons, personal and political, Schmidt believed he had every reason not to rush headlong into an affirmative decision. One of Schmidt's aides summarized Bonn's attitude in mid-September: "We are not going to invite deployment—before your President has even made the decision—and make political fools out of ourselves."[50]

NOTES

1. Helmut Schmidt, *Defense or Retaliation: A German View* (New York: Praeger, 1962), p. 98.

2. Walter Pincus, Washington *Post*, June 6, 1977.

3. From USIA "Neutron Bomb Announcement," Foreign Media Reaction, Current Issues 30, July 14, 1977, p. 5.

4. Ibid, p. 6.

5. Ibid, p. 5.

6. Ibid, p. 7.

7. "Lightning Flash over the Elbe," *Der Spiegel*, July 8, 1977, pp. 19-27.

8. USIA, p. 6.

9. Ibid, p. 7.

10. Ibid.

11. Ibid, p. 4.

12. *Neue Westfaelische*, from USIA, p. 6.

13. "Lightning Flash over the Elbe."

14. Ibid.

15. Theo Sommer, "The Neutron Bomb: Nuclear War Without Tears?" *Survival* 19 (November-December 1977): 263, reprinted from *Die Zeit*, July 29, 1977.

16. Egon Bahr, "Ist die Menschheit dabei, verruckt zu werden?" *Vorwärts*, July 21, 1977.

17. Hans Gerlach, "Neutron Bomb Overshadows Nuclear Arms Limitation Hopes," *German Tribune*, July 31, 1977, p. 3.

18. CSU-Presse, Mitteilungen, No. 342/1977, July 19, 1977, and No. 355/1977, July 26, 1977; CDU/CSU Pressdienst, July 19, 1977.

19. Sommer, p. 263.

20. Sommer, p. 265.

21. Ibid.

22. Sommer, p. 266.

23. Sommer, p. 265.

24. Ellen Lentz, New York *Times*, July 24, 1977.

25. Ibid.

26. Sommer, p. 265.

27. John Dornberg, "In Germany, A Blowup over the Neutron Bomb," *Philadelphia Inquirer*, August 3, 1977, p. 3.

28. Michael Getler, Washington *Post* July 24, 1977, p. 6.

29. Dornberg, p. 3.

30. Lothar Ruehl, *Die Zeit*, August 1977.

31. Ibid.

32. Kurt Sontheimer, *The Government and Politics of West Germany* (London: Hutchison University Library, 1972), p. 95.

33. Manfred Worner, "NATO Defenses and Tactical Nuclear Weapons," *Strategic Review*, Fall 1977, p. 11.

34. Ibid, p. 15.

35. Ibid, p. 16.

36. "CDU-Experte gegen Neutronenbombe," *Stuttgarter Zeitung*, August 26, 1977.

37. Dornberg, p. 3.

38. Hans W. Gatzke, *Germany and the United States: A "Special Relationship"?* (Cambridge, Mass: Harvard University Press, 1980), p. 231.

39. David P. Conradt, *The German Polity* (New York: Longman, 1978), p. 88.

40. Bahr, Vorwärts, July 21, 1977.

41. Rudiger Moniac, "Koschnick furchtet verstarkte Spannungsgefahren," *Die Welt*, July 21, 1977.

42. Ibid.

43. Erhard Morbitz, "SPD—Abgeordneter Pawelczyk greift NATO—Oberbefehlshaber an," *Frankfurter Rundschau*, July 22, 1977.

44. *International Herald Tribune*, July 25, 1977.

45. Conradt, p. 87.

46. Ibid.

47. Michael Getler, "No Bonn Bar Seen to Neutron Arms," *International Herald Tribune*, September 28, 1977.

48. Ibid.

49. Alex Vardamis, "German-American Military Fissures," *Foreign Policy* 34 (Spring 1979): 90.

50. Getler, "No Bonn Bar Seen," *International Herald Tribune*, September 28, 1977.

5

Different Approaches
to Different Problems

This chapter examines the efforts of the Alliance to cope with the neutron bomb after it had been acknowledged as a problem that had to be solved. The Washington bureaucracy plays the largest role, as the initiator of various alternatives for persuading the allies to support deployment of the weapon. The chapter covers events from September through December 1977. This period has been characterized by American participants as the "tilt" phase: modest pressure was applied on the allied leaders to agree to decision making by consensus. Unlike past decisions within the Alliance, the United States refused to make a unilateral decision to produce the weapons until the allies made a public commitment to deploy them. To understand why the usual decision making process in the Alliance was altered we must look to the decision-making process in Washington.

The administration never adopted a formal procedure for handling the neutron bomb issue. The president's indecisiveness prevented him from either delegating responsibility for the issue to his advisors or taking charge himself. Thus policy formulation was informal and erratic. The administration was never fully united on one course of action, but certain senior advisors took the initiative in developing a political strategy for handling the issue.

Allied consultations during fall 1977 were inconclusive. Both Washington and Bonn wanted firmer assurances that the other would uphold its part of the agreement. Washington would not authorize production until Bonn was committed to deployment. Similarly, Bonn would not endorse deployment until Washington was irrevocably committed to produce the weapons.

In November, Washington officials began to search for other approaches to the ERW issue. The administration informally reached the conclusion that

considering ERWs in an arms control framework would enable the Europeans to agree to deployment and would prompt Carter to authorize production. But disagreement within the administration over this maneuver prevented its immediate proposal to the allies. By December, mounting pressure in Europe to resolve the conflict and a highly effective propaganda campaign by the Soviet Union caused the administration to intensify its efforts to reach agreement on production and deployment of ERWs.

FORMULATION OF AMERICAN POLICY ON THE NEUTRON BOMB

In the past, the United States had taken the lead on decisions for nuclear weapons in Europe, and the allies, in general, endorsed America's stewardship. The last major attempt at multilateral decision making, for the Multi-Lateral Force (MLF) in 1965, had ended in disaster and contributed to France's withdrawal from NATO. The United States learned its lesson from this episode and had, for 12 years, endeavored to lead nuclear decisions without appearing to force the Europeans' hand. The ERW case, then, represented a departure from the traditional American approach to alliance consultation and decision making. This conceptual shift was not merely the result of the new and, for the most part, inexperienced American officials involved in the controversy. The post-Watergate, anti-Republican, anti-unilateral sentiment on which the Carter administration was swept into office played a large role in shaping the conceptual context in which the administration approached alliance relations.

In September 1977 the Carter administration came to the conclusion that concrete action had to be taken to resolve the controversy that was continuing to mount over ERWs. The Special Coordinating Committee (SCC) of the NSC thrashed out the possible options during a September meeting. This cabinet-level body, convening in a basement chamber of the White House west wing, was a forum for interagency discussions of important policy matters. Brzezinski was the chairman, although his deputy, David Aaron, sometimes sat in for him. The secretaries of state, defense, and energy, or their deputies, along with representatives of the Arms Control and Disarmament Agency, the Joint Chiefs of Staff, and the intelligence community, sat around a boardroom table with their technical experts seated behind them along the wall. SALT was a prominent issue on the agenda; but as transatlantic tensions over ERWs mounted, the SCC became concerned that European hostility to the weapon would further complicate Europe's reception of SALT. Given the political risks involved in a first commitment by either the United States or the Federal Republic, the majority of SCC members preferred a "damage-limiting" political strategy, one that would be the easiest to obtain on both sides of the Atlantic.

This approach would involve subtle encouragement by the United States, through diplomatic channels and alliance forums, to convince the allies that the simplest way out for all was to reach a consensus within NATO on a European commitment to permit deployment of ERWs in Europe. The declared objective was to prevent the Soviet Union from exploiting differences in the Alliance through a voracious propaganda campaign. In addition, high-level officials in the new administration were worried about the "black marks" this event could leave on the reputation of the new president as an outsider unable to manage affairs in Washington.

Those who, like Cyrus Vance, were personally inclined to reject ERWs on military grounds, altered their stated positions for political reasons. As secretary of state, Vance felt that the weapon's marginal contribution to deterrence in Europe might not outweigh its political liabilities in U.S.-European diplomatic relations. But the persuasiveness of the counterarguments by the other secretaries, combined with Vance's impression that support of ERWs would enhance the credibility of U.S. defense policy in the eyes of an increasingly conservative American public, brought Vance around to the majority opinion. Moreover, he believed that if Brzezinski was supporting a policy that would move toward deployment, it must be the president's preferred option. Vance possessed the lawyerly quality of being able to rally around what he thought was the president's decision even if he would have chosen another option himself. Vance's position is an example of what Allison has called the "51-49" principle.[1] Because participants in a bureacratic "game" must compete with others, a reasonable "player" will often argue for a position he has chosen reluctantly with much more confidence than if he were a detached judge. Vance was a good "team player" in this case; he would be a persuasive advocate of ERW deployment, to the extent that warnings from his staff against the "consensus" approach went unheeded.

With respect to the way the issue would be handled with the Europeans, Vance and Brown led the SCC deliberations in believing that the issue should not be "rammed down the throats of the allies."[2] They agreed that the United States should defer somewhat to the Europeans to give them a sense of contributing to the decisionmaking process. In the secretaries' opinion, this attitude would not only show the Europeans that Washington respected allied opinions, but it would also ease the burden of the president's responsibilities, thereby prompting him to give his strong support to production of ERWs. They rejected heavy-handed persuasion of the allies, out of acute awareness of the potentially disastrous political consequences, especially in Bonn, after the recent strains of SALT on Alliance relations.[3]

The SCC finally agreed on a strategy of applying delicate but persistent pressure on the Europeans, in an effort to prompt them to accept some of the responsibilities of the decision. The allies would be asked for a consensus on deployment at the upcoming meeting of NATO's Nuclear Planning Group in

for deployment, and tried to downplay the domestic political concerns with which the allies, as well as the United States, were preoccupied. The United States hoped the issue could be resolved as a military problem with minor political maneuvering. The military rationales included arguments about improved deterrence, lower collateral damage, better security, and so on. As an aside, the United States added that it would be easier for the allies to deploy the weapons than to hand the Soviets a political and psychological "victory" by seeming to back down in the face of a fierce propaganda campaign by Moscow.

The overt disunity in the Alliance was developing into an irresistable propaganda campaign for the Soviets. In July they had called the weapons a "diabolical toy" of the capitalist warmongers, and now, in September, Foreign Minister Gromyko was asking the United Nations to outlaw plans for neutron weapons. In typical Soviet fashion, he ignored developments of new Soviet weaponry, such as the SS-20, but lambasted the United States: "Can one really propose with one hand various 'drastic reductions' [in SALT] while with the other one authorize the development of new and, bluntly speaking, merciless types of weapons such as the neutron bomb?"[4] Yet Moscow may have harbored some genuine fear of ERWs to the extent that it believed both its own rhetoric and the sensationalism of the Western press. The Soviets may have believed that their tank superiority in Europe would be neutralized by the combination of technological advances in conventional weaponry in the West and the possible deployment of the neutron bomb. Western media exacerbated Soviet concerns by overemphasizing the ability of the neutron weapons to correct the 3:1 tank superiority of the Warsaw Pact, the importance of which became evident only when the weapon's proponents stressed military rationales to justify their political objectives.

Discussion within the SCC of the impact of Soviet propaganda on the ability of the Alliance to reach a mutual agreement in favor of deployment left American officials with the impression that the greater the intensity of Soviet criticism, the more plausible arguments for deployment as a form of resistance to Soviet threats would appear to the Europeans. SCC members felt that Soviet pressure would aid their political strategy by forcing NATO to demonstrate the cohesiveness of the Alliance.[5] By September the United States had incorporated into its policy the assumption that Soviet propaganda would serve Western ends more than Moscow's objective of "driving a wedge between the allies." Although this analysis may have been correct in the long-run, this view precluded American efforts to minimize the impact of Soviet propaganda upon European public opinion, and hence upon the positions adopted by their governments.

By not responding immediately to Soviet propaganda with similar denunciations of their new weapons systems, such as the SS-20, and in publicly stating that the allies would have to join in the decision-making process, the United States miscalculated the effects of public decision making for nuclear

policy on the Europeans. European leaders tend to believe that discussions of and decisions on this type of sensitive military and political issue should be kept more discreet and in private channels than the Carter administration believed possible. After congressional demands for public debate and for public statements from European leaders on their positions, the administration felt committed to an open decision-making process, where transatlantic exchanges would be public transactions. Domestic pressures, such as those from Congress, decisively shaped the administration's political strategy for handling ERWs. But European governments are not as comfortable as their American counterparts with exposing sensitive nuclear matters to public scrutiny. Different perceptions of nuclear decision making are partially a function of the different roles of the press and of parliaments on the two continents. While Europeans cannot comprehend the constitutional inability of the United States to limit the power of the press, the United States underestimates the responsibility of parliamentary governments to political parties.

Following interagency deliberations in September, American policy focused on how to handle European opinion. State department negotiators worked on constructing a salable case for deployment for their European counterparts. As the United States proceeded, alternative options for not deploying ERWs slowly vanished from the range of feasible considerations. Alternative options to deployment were rapidly eliminated in practical scenarios, if not in theory. The option of declaring unilaterally not to produce ERWs was ruled out as a move that would be damaging to the president's leadership on foreign policy matters, not because production was the only way to alleviate intraalliance tension. Thereafter, many working-level U.S. officials who might have been opposed to deployment remained silent. Given the mounting criticism in Congress of Carter's decision to cancel the B-1 bomber and of SALT II, a unilateral decision to scrap the neutron bomb would have been interpreted, by critics whose support was crucial to the ratification of SALT, as another case of ignoring the Soviet threat.

Although Carter had not put his signature to any of the plans, the administration assumed it was carrying out his wishes. Why did this mysterious lack of communication go unattended for several months? A partial answer is Carter's reluctance to give his senior advisors a clear idea of the outcome he desired. The other part of the answer concerns the procedures by which a decision of this nature is handled by the bureaucracy. The political strategy for moving in concert with the allies toward a joint decision on production and deployment had emerged from the deliberations of the SCC. Whatever planning occurred to arrive at this strategy was informal. The SCC is not a formal decision-making body; it is a forum for interagency discussion and exchange. But no one organization was charged with "having the action," a bureaucratic term referring to the individual or organization responsible for moving an issue through the government and for taking the initiative in

drafting whatever papers are to go to the president.[6] The "action" on ERWs fell by default to Brzezinski and the NSC, primarily because Brzezinski was chairman of the SCC and he alone was willing to assume responsibility for the issue. The neutron bomb was an issue most bureacrats wanted to avoid. No one in the administration, from the outset of the controversy, thought that the neutron bomb would be remembered as one of the administration's foreign policy successes. Thus, as former Secretary of State Dean Rusk noted, "power gravitates to those who are willing to make decisions and live with the results."[7] Brzezinski was the one senior official with a drive for power. His assumption of responsibility was credible to other senior officials not only because they preferred not to bear the burden of potential "failure," but also because Brzezinski had the confidence of the president. The president's confidence in his National Security advisor was likely to have led Carter to trust Brzezinski with handling the neutron bomb issue at this stage of the game. The president's characteristic of "uncommitted thinking" combined with Carter's own personal dilemma about nuclear arms reinforced his confidence in Brzezinski's competence on this matter. Brzezinski's knowledge of the trust reposed in him led him to believe that a resolute demonstration of his willingness to assume responsibility would enable him to win the support of other key officials and thereby prompt the president to make a decision to go ahead with production and deployment.

AN INCONCLUSIVE OCTOBER

Now supposedly settled on a course of action, the administration hoped to get the ERW problem out of the way as quickly as possible. The United States would seek to settle the issue at the upcoming biannual meeting of NATO's Nuclear Planning Group, scheduled for October 11 and 12 in Bari, Italy. Preliminary efforts were required. The first step was to try to coax assurances of deployment from allied leaders prior to the NPG meeting so that full agreement could be made public at Bari. The United States accorded high priority to a show of Alliance unity at these formal meetings, not only for the sake of intra-Alliance rapport but also because SALT negotiations were at a delicate pitch in early September and a show of disunity might damage the West's bargaining position. Thus in preparation for the Bari meeting a series of multilateral and bilateral meetings were scheduled, through which the United States hoped to iron out misunderstandings and convince the allies to come forward with a public declaration supporting deployment.

One such meeting was a visit by Brzezinski to Chancellor Schmidt on September 27. The chancellor told Brzezinski that he was willing to deploy the weapons on German soil if two conditions were met: one, that Carter first announce his intent to produce ERWs, and second, that NATO as a whole

agree that they are necessary and should be stockpiled in West Germany.[8] In Bonn's view, NATO consultations were essential to provide an allied rather than a U.S.-West German stance on the situation. Domestic pressures were clearly exacting a toll on Schmidt's government: "We are not going to invite deployment—before your President has even made that decision—and make political fools out of ourselves," a German official told an American reporter.[9] Another aide to Schmidt added that the West Germans "don't want to give an answer before it is decided by the President to produce the weapons."[10] Schmidt's first condition ran counter to U.S. plans, which, as formulated earlier that month, implicitly assumed that either Bonn would make the first public commitment or agreement would be reached in private channels so that the decisions on production and deployment could be announced simultaneously. Inside the Carter administration, officials reacted with dismay to Brzezinski's visit. The Germans are "hedging the issue, playing it close to their vests," remarked one participant. Bonn wanted the United States to bear the burden of decision, with no strings attached to Europe for deployment. This attitude left Bonn and Washington, the two most important links in NATO's defense posture, locked in a "which comes first, the chicken or the egg" situation on the subject of publicly endorsing ERWs.[11]

The administration had clearly underestimated the constraints on European leaders. The reaction in Washington to Brzezinski's meeting with Schmidt was to postpone a decision until after further consultations in NATO. Washington was clearly troubled by Schmidt's conditions but hoped that if other allies would express their approval, Schmidt would see the light and lead an European endorsement. American expectations of an allied agreement had declined since Schmidt's announcement that he would withhold his endorsement until Carter made his decision; therefore, the United States declined to formally include the issue on the agenda for the Bari meeting.[12] The United States hoped that by allaying European fears of alleged American willingness to limit the range of the cruise missile in SALT, an important concern in NATO, agreement on neutron weapons would be easier to achieve.

The two-day meeting of the NPG ended without allied agreement on the neutron bomb. The NPG is composed of seven NATO members: the United States, Federal Republic of Germany, Britain, and Italy hold permanent seats; Belgium, Denmark, and Greece then held the three rotating positions. Brown opened the meeting with remarks on the nuclear balance in Europe and the latest strategic developments in the United States, including plans to produce a new intercontinental missile, the MX. He then urged the allies to share responsibility with the United States for the ERW and asserted that it would be produced only if the Europeans made the first public commitment. In effect, he threw the burden of decision into the hands of the allies, leaving them confused about American intentions. They wondered how much Washington really wanted this weapon, if it was unwilling to make a commitment to produce it.

Brown told them that a European "consensus," but not "unanimity," was required and that the United States would "continue to sound out the views of its allies."[13] He added that the United States would refrain from exerting undue pressure on Europe; the weapons would "not be rammed down the throats" of the allies.[14] But this type of forceful persuasion was exactly the sort of pressure that allied leaders needed to free themselves from domestic opposition. If the United States had played its traditional role, European governments could have consented to deployment in private consultations and defended this position in public by relying on American support. Without this support, European governments would face unmitigated Soviet propaganda, the purpose of which was to divide the Alliance. In order to give some semblance of agreement, in spite of political disunity, the NPG issued a public statement that "there is general agreement on the military and deterrent effect of such weapons. . . ."[15] But such agreement was unsuccessful in hiding the political differences on a decision that now had little to do with the weapon itself but concerned how the decision would be made and who would make it.

The United States wanted a European consensus that appeared impossible to achieve. Italy, for example, claimed it had not received prior notification of the American proposal and therefore expected the NPG meeting to be an informative rather than a deliberative session. When pressed for information on Italy's reaction to the U.S. proposals by members of the Chamber of Deputies' Foreign Affairs Commission just prior to the NPG meeting, Luciano Radi, undersecretary at the Italian Foreign Ministry, had to acknowledge that the debate had thus far taken place without real information on the nature of the weapon.[16] He told his colleagues that the government had not as yet taken a stand on the issue as the problem "must be carefully analysed inside the proper circles."[17] Italy and the Netherlands were noncommittal, in large part because public opinion strongly opposed deployment of the neutron bomb with Italian and Dutch forces. Denmark and Norway had no intention of altering their traditional policy of avoiding any nuclear role in NATO. Belgium also declined to take a stand.

After West Germany, Britain was the next most important European country in a multilateral NATO decision.[18] In asking the allies for a consensus on deployment, Brown had stressed that most weight would be given to the views of those countries "on whose territory the weapons would be deployed,"[19] or those who maintain forces in West Germany equipped with nuclear-capable artillery, such as the British Army on the Rhine. Although Britain also refused to take a position at the October meeting, government officials acknowledged that the Labour government could be expected to acquiesce in either an American or German decision but would not attempt to lead a European consensus. As a warhead designed for an artillery shell with a maximum range of 13 miles and for the Lance missile with a range of 70 miles, ERWs would serve no purpose on British soil. Since ERWs would be deployed

only with British troops stationed in West Germany, neutron weapons were not vital to British national security. Furthermore, in the roles played by the United States and Britain in their traditional "special relationship," the United States was expected to lead on most bilateral as well as Alliance matters. As long as the United States was seen to exhibit a modicum of leadership the British government was content to follow the American example.

But the Labour government, led by Prime Minister James Callaghan, faced domestic opposition to the neutron weapon almost as virulent as that on the Continent. It is important to remember that the European press gathered its information from American media, often leading to double distortion by the time the news appeared in print in Europe. Misinformation added to the emotional public debate, which was directed to a large extent by vocal antinuclear groups, such as the Campaign for Nuclear Disarmament.[20] Moreover, the government found it difficult to counter irrational criticism or allay the public's fears, either because the government itself lacked adequate information or because it was reluctant to disseminate what it knew for fear that it would be forced to take a firm position. Although during the fall the Ministry of Defence and the Foreign Office did launch a moderately successful campaign to improve the neutron bomb's public image by briefing members of the press, the damage to public opinion had already been done.

Probably the most important reason for the Labour government's delay in adopting an official position was dissension within the ranks of the party. Faced with the prospect of an election the following year, 1978, the Labour Party wanted to avoid irritating a vocal minority within its ranks that opposed the neutron concept.[21] A faction of the left wing of the Labour Party took a doctrinal opposition to all nuclear weapons, urging Britain to dismantle its nuclear weapons and withdraw from NATO. Although this faction was a minority in 1977, its power was on the rise, as witnessed in the party's 1980 platform and its leadership in 1981. Left-wing members of the party, such as Labour MP Robin Cook, attacked Defence Minister Fred Mulley and the Defense Ministry for not playing a larger role in educating parliamentarians and the public about neutron weapons.[22] The political effort required to rally the Labour Party to a government position in favor of deployment was much more difficult than if the Conservatives, lacking an equivalent faction, had been in power.

Defence Minister Mulley would be responsible for defending the government's official position in public. He would have to quell growing opposition from Labour's back bench. Mulley, an elderly man with a long party tradition, was known to many as a "senior Labour old-boy" who valued highly the party's support of his positions and policies. Mulley was prepared to follow British tradition by acquiescing in an American decision and felt that this was the extent of Britain's responsibility in the matter. As for his personal view of the weapon, Mulley was more concerned with the potentially adverse

political impact on his party leadership than with the weapon's military utility. He needed to be persuaded that the political risks involved in backing the United States were worth any military benefits the weapon could offer to NATO's defense posture. By late October he had apparently been won over by the military rationales for the weapon.[23]

Foreign Minister David Owen, however, was more skeptical than Mulley of the weapon's purported military value. A dedicated arms controller, Owen's primary concern was not the weapon's contribution to NATO's force posture but rather its impact on ongoing arms control talks, such as MBFR and SALT, and on the political process of détente. He was certainly not pleased with the assessment of ACDA's report to Congress that the arms control impact of ERWs would be "marginally negative." His doubts about the political practicality of supporting ERWs probably increased after his effusive reception in Moscow by Brezhnev in October.[24] Owen's doubts may have constrained the government from taking an official position during the summer and early fall; however, by the end of the year the government formally stated that it would support an American decision for production and deployment.

The West Germans, like the British, concurred with Brown's favorable military assessment of the neutron weapon but were also unwilling to make a formal public commitment on deployment. Although Defense Minister Georg Leber agreed that ERWs would strengthen NATO's deterrent capability by making it easier for the Germans to contemplate using TNWs on their soil, he tied a German commitment to deploy the neutron bomb to simultaneous deployment by at least one other European ally. He also suggested that the weapon might be useful as a "bargaining chip" in an arms control forum.[25] With Brezhnev expected to visit Bonn in November, the Schmidt government was undoubtedly reluctant to upset the delicate balance of East-West détente at that time.

Thus the outcome of the Bari NPG meeting did not produce the results for which the United States had hoped: an agreement on conditions for deployment in Europe. Each government withheld a position in one way or another with a good deal of equivocation showing through in the final communiqué: Belgium did "not wish to make its definitive opinion known"; Italy did "not wish to adopt a position"; and Germany and Britain were "not formally opposed."[26] Washington explained somewhat defensively that Brown's proposals had enabled the allies to maintain a workable dialogue on the matter. Some administration officials were relieved that Brown had successfully placed the responsibility for the decision in a multilateral framework, and thus reduced the political burden on Washington. Richard Burt, then national security correspondent for the New York *Times*, said that he was aware that "the Carter Administration and the President himself seemed to be implicity moving away from the unilateral responsibilities of the United States to a pluralist model of Alliance decision making."[27] Perhaps

without realizing the full implications of the change, the administration was skating onto thin ice: Carter

> asked the Europeans, particularly the Germans, to play a role which they were unprepared to play. . . . Not simply unprepared in the sense that Schmidt didn't like the fact that he had to stand up to American nuclear power, but that German political society could not, and cannot still, join the United States in a nuclear partnership on equal footing.[28]

In retrospect, it seems clear that if the United States had been more forceful with the Europeans, the latter would have found it politically easier to comply with Washington's wishes. But at the time many of the negotiators in the State Department believed, or wanted to believe, that the issue would quietly dissipate without aggressive American action because the political costs of public disagreement within NATO were too great on both sides of the Atlantic. This assumption gained credibility by default as a consensus within the administration on what to do next became harder and harder to achieve. Carter did not get actively involved in the diplomatic tactics or political maneuvers, leaving the NSC to toe the policy line. While Brown and Brzezinski favored deployment and thought that the Europeans should be brought into the decision, some of Brzezinski's assistants were convinced that the allies would be unwilling to bear their share of the burden. Moreover, several NSC members were fundamentally opposed to the weapon itself but were not in a position to challenge Brzezinski and actually kill the program. They could, however, employ delaying tactics, such as withholding information, to stall concerted action. This subtle undermining of an internal consensus went well with the attitude of a number of State Department officials who felt that the Alliance could as easily live without ERWs as it could afford to strain its principal partners and their relations with each other over such a minor military matter.

Another factor preventing decisive action by the administration was internal concern about upsetting the SALT process. American SALT negotiators, many of whom were also given responsibility for "working the neutron bomb issue," were reluctant to propose action that might either diminish their bargaining position in SALT by appearing to back down in the face of Soviet criticism or so aggravate Moscow that compromises in SALT would be impossible. Furthermore, these officials did agree that the present SALT negotiations were already so politically taxing for the Europeans that the interjection of another issue would only aggravate an already strained U.S.-European dialogue. As there was considerable overlap between the American officials who would ultimately shape U.S. policy with regard to both limiting strategic arms and deploying neutron arms, these officials had a personal and bureaucratic interest in keeping the path for the conclusion of a SALT agreement as clear as possible.

But the option of postponing a decision on ERWs was quickly foreclosed by the increasing intensity of Soviet criticism. Soviet propaganda so impinged on the European's attitudes that many administration officials who had originally been opposed to the weapon had to defend the device to fend off what they saw as "absurd criticism," with the consequence that they appeared to shift to a political position in favor of deployment. As Soviet public outrage increased, it became harder for the United States to defuse the issue. Eventually the United States would blame Moscow for making it impossible for the Alliance to "put the issue on the back burner."

CAN ARMS CONTROL HIDE WEAPONS ACQUISITION?

In November 1977 the major obstacle Washington saw to production and deployment of the neutron bomb was the inability of European governments to overcome Soviet criticism and public opposition. Neither Soviet propaganda nor European public opinion could be silenced by arguments extolling the weapon's military virtues. One of the major objections to ERWs in both Moscow and Western Europe was that arms control negotiations (MBFR and SALT) would be undermined by the introduction of a weapon that appeared inappropriate both for the predominantly conventional arms control forum (MBFR) and for strategic arms limitation (SALT). During the Bari meeting the United States realized that the nature of the issue demanded a "political decision,"[29] with tactics that needed to be more politically persuasive than militarily sound. Thus Washington began to look seriously at its political strategy from another perspective: consideration of ERWs within an arms control framework.

Putting military considerations aside, a decision to produce and deploy ERWs was likely to have a negative impact across a variety of U.S. arms control initiatives. First, deployment of the neutron weapon would weaken the prospects for achieving an MBFR agreeement: *Novosti*, the Soviet News Agency, had cautioned that the neutron bomb was "an attempt to undermine the basis on which understanding at the Vienna force reduction talks should be founded."[30] The weapon might also intensify pressures on Moscow to increase its troop and armored deployments in Eastern Europe, since the ERW would be targeted against its conventional forces. Second, a commitment to produce and deploy a new nuclear warhead would require further testing, reducing the prospects for agreement on a Comprehensive Test Ban (CTB) treaty. Third, an American decision to deploy ERWs might call into question the sincerity of American efforts for nuclear nonproliferation.[31] Fourth, the deployment would adversely affect the climate of the SALT talks.

Thus Washington began to wonder whether considering ERWs in an arms control framework might actually enable the allies to agree to deployment by

quelling European public opposition and quieting Soviet criticism. This was a purely political tactic, devised by the weapon's supporters to bolster the rationale for deployment. There was no intention whatsoever of halting the deployment of the weapon in exchange for a concession from Moscow because, as we shall see, Washington expected Moscow to refuse any offer the United States might propose. This maneuver is a true case of arms control as a "fig leaf"[32] to hide weapons acquisition and is one reason (the failure of SALT being another) why analysts would soon be lamenting that arms control, as a process, had failed.[33]

Several occurrences in fall 1977 provided impetus for this approach to the deployment of ERWs and convinced many Washington officials that the Europeans would actually welcome this political maneuver. First, on October 28 Schmidt gave a major speech at the International Institute for Strategic Studies in London, attracting unusual attention for his suggestion that the West apply arms control measures "to all weapons," by which he was referring to all nuclear weapons not included in SALT. He also addressed the neutron bomb issue, arguing that

> we have to examine whether the neutron weapons are of value to the Alliance as an additional element of the deterrence strategy, as a means of preventing war, but we . . . also should examine what relevance and weight this weapon has in regard to our efforts to achieve arms control.[34]

Second, in mid-October 1977, in the midst of the heated German debate, former Chancellor Willy Brandt submitted a widely read paper entitled "Theses on Disarmament" to a meeting of the Socialist International, a group of Social Democratic and Socialist parties in the West and in Third World countries who had elected Brandt chairman of the group in 1976. In referring to the so-called gray-area weapons that were not dealt with either at SALT or at MBFR, Brandt also indicated that arms control negotiations should be extended to include those systems:

> Before a decision on new qualitative weapons systems is made, careful consideration should be given to the consequences on the policy of detente and arms control negotiations. . . . In this context the so-called neutron weapon should be considered . . . decisions on armaments have to consider besides the military-strategic deliberations also the justified fears of the citizens.[35]

Third, at an SPD convention on November 15, Schmidt's party passed a resolution instructing him "to create the conditions that would ensure that the deployment of the neutron weapon in Germany is not necessary."[36] While the

American president is, in many ways, unconstrained by his party's platform, the Federal chancellor must heed his party's resolutions or risk defections from his party.

Finally, in the Netherlands, where much of the population has tradition-ally been opposed to all forms of nuclear weaponry, the government, on November 7, held a public hearing on neutron weapons, at which defense experts from Europe and the United States provided testimony. Most of the participants, among them Daniel Ellsberg, were firmly opposed to the deployment of the neutron bomb in Europe. The Dutch government con-cluded that it would not participate in a European consensus to deploy the weapon. The government seems to have agreed most with the testimony of German General Graf von Baudissin, who recommended that the best course of action would be "to postpone the production of enhanced radiation weapons and to introduce the project as a bargaining chip in negotiations."[37] Unlike the United States, however, the Dutch wanted to halt the deployment of ERWs in exchange for an equitable Soviet concession.

In Washington officials agreed that the present situation of mutual postponement in order to avoid public blame was unsatisfactory. Resolution of the issue was not in sight, and the West was becoming psychologically defensive. Action had to be taken to relieve the pressure on allied governments and to defuse the extensive scrutiny of Western weapons modernization by the Soviets. By offering to limit deployment of ERWs in exchange for a concession from Moscow, the burden of decision, Washington hoped, would be placed squarely on the shoulders of the Soviets, rather than in the hands of the Europeans. Such an approach might free both the United States and Europe from the weight of domestic opposition.

What Use Is a Bargaining Chip?

The idea of using a bargaining chip approach to ERWs was probably first raised at the September meeting of the Special Coordinating Committee as a means to overcome the impasse to an allied decision on deployment.[38] Such a proposal might relieve both the American government and its NATO allies from making a decision on an issue that was fraught with controversy, sensitivity, and public concern. It would halt Soviet efforts to exploit the ERW issue for propagandistic purposes. It would underline the sincerity of American efforts to work toward a limitation of armaments. By removing one cause of friction from East-West negotiations, it might improve the international political climate and thereby possibly contribute to and increase the chances for reaching arms control agreements. By providing an additional bargaining chip, it might help to quiet the criticisms of West Europeans who had argued that the United States bargained away the cruise missile for selfish reasons in the Protocol to the SALT II draft in September. It would also appease

European opponents of the weapon. At the same time, such an offer would put the Soviet Union, having exaggerated the importance of ERWs, on the defensive if it objected to making concessions in return for a mutual agreement not to deploy the neutron weapon. But of the various proposals considered in Washington, U.S. officials expected that none of them would be acceptable to the Soviet Union. That was the whole idea: after the Soviets rejected the phony arms control offer, Western governments would no longer be blamed for deploying the weapons. Moscow would be seen as the culprit in escalating the arms race, not NATO.

What Kind of Arms Control Offer?

Normally an arms control offer is decided upon at the end of an analytic study. No interagency analysis was conducted on arms control options for ERWs. The first arms control proposal—to include ERWs in negotiations under way in Vienna for the mutual reduction of Eastern and Western forces in Central Europe—was, in all likelihood, an impromptu idea thrown out for consideration in early fall 1977 to increase the range of alternatives available to the United States for managing this controversial issue.

Although some State Department and ACDA officials were attracted to what was known as the "MBFR option," many others, with more political clout, pointed out the inadequacies of introducing ERWs as a bargaining chip into Vienna's highly stylized, highly bureaucratized arms control forum. First, a proposal on ERWs would add to the already heavy demands on Eastern Europe, particularly in the complex section known as "option 3," which concerns nuclear weapons in Europe. Second, a public declaration of willingness to limit deployment of ERWs within MBFR would place a restriction on qualitative improvements to NATO's tactical nuclear forces, at a time when the allies were in the midst of agreeing to a Long-Term Defense Plan, part of which specified improvement of just such forces. Third, the limitation of ERWs would be unverifiable—surveillance techniques cannot distinguish between an "ordinary" nuclear warhead and one with enhanced radiation features—whereas other categories of weapons and forces being discussed in Vienna conformed to the principle of verifiability. Fourth, the limitation of equipment in MBFR had always been more difficult to achieve than restrictions on manpower. But most important of all, any trade-off on ERWs in MBFR would be "asymmetrical"; in other words, the Warsaw Pact could not offer to limit any similar weapons systems, as it did not possess ERWs. Since a major principle of the Vienna talks at that time was "symmetrical reduction," both American negotiators in Vienna and Warsaw Pact representatives could be expected to reject any such offer out of hand, alleging that the United States was not sincerely committed to arms control and merely wanted to upset the already tenuous state of negotiations.

Many ACDA and State Department officials who genuinely believed in the process of arms control were disturbed by the suggestion that ERWs might further complicate MBFR and made various proposals that they thought presented the administration with better alternatives. An aide to ACDA's director, Paul Warnke, suggested that the United States and the Soviet Union publicly proclaim a moratorium on the production of neutron weapons, after which the United States could obtain, through private negotiations a more substantive *quid pro quo* beneficial to arms control. This aide was not convinced of the military utility of ERWs; he viewed them as at best "marginally effective" and at worst as "politically damaging." Furthermore, his immediate concern as an ACDA official was the upcoming UN Conference on Disarmament in May 1978. A moratorium on ERW production could have provided a convenient way out of a difficult political situation in which the United States risked being accused of disregarding the nuclear Non-Proliferation Treaty (NPT), many of whose signatories would be attending the UN conference.

Although Warnke may not have agreed with his aide's recommendation, he was a devout believer in the positive aims of arms control for the limitation both of weapons acquisition and of nuclear proliferation. In testimony before the Senate Foreign Relations Committee in 1974 he had opposed the introduction of "mini-nukes" into NATO's tactical nuclear arsenals. He had argued that by making the consequences of the use of TNWs less dire to the potential attacker, they were a less effective deterrent than the TNWs presently stockpiled in Europe.[39] Warnke knew that ERWs alone did not offer serious arms control possibilities and that their asymmetries with existing arms control forums would only aggravate present complications in both arenas, MBFR and SALT. If at all possible, he would not want phony arms control measures to "corrupt" the true nature of the process itself, thereby weakening prospects for concluding arms control agreements. But Warnke had to worry about his own professional interests, which at the time may have been better served by staying out of a bureaucratic battle over ERWs. Mistrusted by conservatives for allegedly being "soft" on the Soviet Union, Warnke may have foreseen further antagonism with his colleagues if he vociferously objected to ERWs. Moreover, influencing Carter's approach to SALT was infinitely more important than worrying over a weapon as "marginal" as ERWs. If he could not do both, he would certainly choose SALT.

Objections were also brewing in the State Department. An aide to Vance sent the secretary of state a memo during the fall recommending that the United States reverse its present course and refrain completely from proceeding with the ERW program. Vance's aide was fundamentally opposed to the neutron weapon and later hung a poster from a Dutch protest against the neutron bomb in his office. This aide felt that the military advantages of ERWs were so marginal that its deployment was not worth the political cost to ongoing arms control negotiations and to Alliance relations in general. In fall

1977 he felt that discontinuation of the program was the preferred "damage-limiting" strategy. In his professional capacity he had more at stake in the diplomatic and political consequences that would follow a major Alliance row over ERWs than he had an interest in a minor improvement to NATO's force posture. But the secretary of state was out of town when the memo reached his desk, and before he had a chance to consider it the Pentagon put forward its proposal on how to handle the neutron bomb. Minor organizational procedures and the arbitrariness of time can have a crucial impact on final outcomes.

While the State Department memo lay waiting in Vance's in-tray, the director of the DoD SALT Task Force, Walter Slocombe, made a connection between SALT and ERW. He authored the proposal that won the approval of Brzezinski and Brown and their staffs and became the administration's preferred course of action. Slocombe's idea was to link a decision on the neutron weapon to Soviet restraint in deploying its new intermediate range ballistic missile known in the West as the SS-20. The SS-20 is a mobile ballistic missile equipped with three independently targetable warheads. In 1977 the Soviet Union had just begun to deploy the SS-20 in its Western Military Districts. Because the SS-20, with an approximate range of 5,000 kilometers, cannot strike targets in the United States, American negotiators had been unable to include it as a strategic weapon in the SALT talks, causing consternation among Europeans, who were its obvious potential targets. Mobile missiles enhance unilateral security but undercut bilateral arms control agreements, because they are harder to find, harder to count, and harder to hit as targets of retaliation. Therefore, both the United States and its NATO allies were particularly worried about this new weapon. Slocombe offered three reasons why the United States should link the deployment of the neutron bomb and the SS-20, none of them related to arms control, but two of them peripheral to SALT: First, the proposal would focus as much attention on Soviet weapons modernization as the Soviets had drawn to Western force improvements. If the proposal were taken seriously, these two weapons, which propaganda efforts had made appear politically important, might be moved to their proper realm of discussion: military significance. Second, the SS-20 option appeared simpler than complicating the difficult problems of symmetry in MBFR by trying to introduce the weapons there. Third, such a suggestion would "make things awkward" for the Soviet Union by forcing them to choose between their highly prized SS-20 and the highly despised ERW. The implicit fourth and most important reason for the offer was to palliate European opposition to ERWs and thus provide more political leverage to European leaders.

But linking the SS-20 and ERW also had its drawbacks. Like the plan for including the neutron weapon in MBFR, the SS-20-ERW link was criticized as a "ridiculous concept" for its "symmetry" problems: one is a launcher for

intermediate-range missiles and the other is a warhead for battlefield use. Furthermore, the trade-off could not be negotiated at either SALT or MBFR because of the asymmetrical nature of the two weapons. Some officials favored the establishment of a third set of East-West arms control negotiations focusing specifically on European nuclear problems.[40] Not until NATO proposed to deploy systems comparable to the SS-20, the Pershing II and cruise missile, would it be possible to establish an arms control forum on European theater nuclear forces. And even so, the current intermediate nuclear force (INF) negotiations were mandated by NATO's 1979 dual-track decision, not by a Soviet desire to negotiate arms reductions.

Some State Department officials regarded Slocombe's proposal as a deliberate ploy by the "SALT people" in the Pentagon and the NSC to turn the growing problem of neutron weapons to their advantage in SALT. These critics attributed the interest of the DoD SALT Task Force in ERWs to their recent recognition that if the issue was not resolved soon, their precious SALT treaty would be in danger. By forcefully advocating the SS-20 proposal, ERW might become a convincing bargaining chip in the U.S.-Soviet dialogue, gathering support for SALT among both European and congressional critics. This proposal, whose implicit objective was not the limitation but the deployment of ERWs, would help to dispel criticism by American conservatives and European nuclearists that the Carter administration was appeasing the Soviets in SALT and lacked forcefulness on defense issues, such as the cancellation of the B-1 bomber had just seemed to demonstrate. On the other hand, to those who took the arms control offer at face value, they might now have greater faith in the administration's commitment to disarmament.

Various solutions to the neutron bomb problem were discussed at the mid-November meeting of the Special Coordinating Committee. The officials who drafted the technical analysis of the MBFR-ERW link were not optimistic about its prospects primarily because verifiable restrictions would be impossible to implement and the American delegation in Vienna was opposed to the introduction of an asymmetrical weapon in their already complicated negotiations. Brzezinski, who chaired this meeting, supported the idea of an arms control offer as a means of obtaining allied agreement, but he was looking for a more informal, one-shot negotiating deal than the MBFR offer. He settled on the SS-20 option as the best method of facilitating an allied decision. NSC and DoD members agreed that since the Bari meeting, when Brown had asked the allies to join in a decision, "the monkey was on the Europeans' back."[41] Now the Soviets would become responsible. The NSC and DoD were also becoming acutely aware of the pressures mounting on their own responsibilities: If Washington could not muster the allies' support, American's bargaining position at SALT would be psychologically weakened, and the administration's capacity for political leadership would be perceptibly tainted, in both Soviet and European eyes. A manifest demonstration of political will was needed.

The scenario that was constructed for the SS-20-ERW arms control offer was the predecessor of NATO's December 1979 dual-track decision to deploy long–range TNFs (theatre nuclear forces) in Europe and to simultaneously negotiate with the Soviets on possible limitations of these systems. American officials would discuss the arms control proposal with the Europeans in private consultations. American proponents of the plan expected that European leaders would find deployment politically acceptable if the Soviets would not agree to limit the SS-20 in exchange for similar limits on ERWs. Washington assumed that Moscow would reject the offer. Soviet leaders would rant and rave about the "capitalist bogey" but they would never exchange their coveted new missile for a mere battlefield warhead. The offer was asymmetrical and nonnegotiable; precisely because it had no genuine possibilities of limiting the arms in question, the offer became the preferred American position.

But the administration was not entirely won over. Carter had not discussed the issue in public since July when he had asked Congress to approve funds for the weapon so that he could keep "his options open." Lacking knowledge of the president's views, some State Department and ACDA officials began to think that Brzezinski, in league with the Pentagon, was trying to formulate foreign policy over the head of the Secretary of State. Disagreements between Vance and Brzezinski were well publicized and their staffs often inadvertently exacerbated the controversy by providing the press with information that reflected their department's preferred position.

Just such interagency conflict and rivalry plagued this episode and many others in the neutron bomb controversy. One 'week after the November SCC meeting at which the various arms control options had been discussed, reporters from the Washington *Post* and the New York *Times* got hold of the story. By now the administration was aware that an allied agreement would have to be achieved through quiet diplomacy, but some officials opposed the plan and were prompted to disclose various pieces of information. The two reporters, Walter Pincus for the Washington *Post* and Richard Burt for the New York *Times*, had different sources in Washington and received information that stressed different aspects of the administration's considerations. Burt, having established a secure line of communication within the NSC, had the more accurate story. He outlined the various arms control alternatives under consideration and hinted that the SS-20 was most likely to be the option chosen. The headline—"U.S. May Offer Soviet Deal Shelving Neutron Bomb"—stressed Burt's conclusion.[42] Pincus, on the other hand, reported only the rejection of the MBFR option and underlined the existence of an interagency conflict. He referred to the disagreements between "sharply divided presidential national security advisors" and proclaimed that the decision not to introduce neutron weapons at MBFR "was a victory for proponents of the new generation of weapons, principally the Pentagon, and some staff members of the NSC."[43] Jody Powell, the president's press secretary, immediately tried to

counter Pincus's allegation, claiming that Pincus's information was based on "leaks . . . evidently designed to influence policy."[44] It was clear that the administration lacked a uniform voice on the issue and could not agree on a single spokesman. To make matters worse, Pincus's article was widely read in Europe, as it was also published in the *International Herald Tribune*.

Consistent with the domestic lenses through which American officials saw the controversy, the SS-20 arms control offer was not tailored to European domestic considerations. West German political requirements precluded the realization of the American scenario for an SS-20-ERW arms control offer as a prelude to deployment. Bonn's principal objections were not to the idea of an arms control offer to facilitate deployment but rather to the order of the scenario. The FRG preferred a formula whereby the United States would make an independent decision to produce ERWs; the acquisition of a new weapon would precipitate the creation of an arms control forum for their limitation; and finally, failing concessions from the Soviet Union, Schmidt, in collaboration with other European leaders, would be in a political position to request deployment. In Bonn's view, the European decision on deployment followed U.S.-Soviet bilateral discussions on arms control. According to Washington's approach, an American production decision and an allied decision on deployment would be agreed to before arms control discussions began, even if the two decisions were not publicly announced together.[45] The administration wanted assurance of a European commitment to deploy because Carter was unwilling to accept the burden alone. Washington assumed the arms control considerations could be discussed in the two-year interim between production starts and actual deployment in Europe.

Senior American officials, like Brzezinski and Brown, were worried about a loss of bargaining power with the Soviets in SALT and a decline in perceived political will and American leadership in NATO. But their biggest problem soon became obtaining the president's support. If they approached him directly at this stage he might scrap the weapon altogether, but Brzezinski had already committed himself to production and deployment and was gathering support both within the administration and in Europe. The preferred style of play seems to have been reticence, which allowed senior officials to avoid discussion with the president until they could present him with a proposal to which the Europeans were firmly committed. Allison has posited that reticence, or hesitant silence, permits each participant "to interpret an outcome in the way in which the shoe pinches least."[46] For Carter, reticence allowed him to defer a decision on the problematic issue until his staff had developed a substantive recommendation. Chancellor Schmidt was also more concerned about domestic political consequences than he was about external threats: Diminished parliamentary support from the left wing of the SPD might bring down his government. In Schmidt's view, any plan for resolving the neutron bomb controversy would have to neutralize the possibility that Bonn would be

the focal point of criticism by the Soviet Union and by European socialists, primarily in the Netherlands, Norway, and Denmark, all of which vociferously opposed deployment in Europe. Opponents in these countries had the virtually unanimous support of sympathetic activist groups in West Germany who accused their government of renewed militarism. To prevent criticism from being directed at Bonn alone, Schmidt wanted assurance that at least one other European ally would agree to deployment.

Furthermore, Schmidt himself had reservations about supporting an arms control offer on a weapon that was neither clearly strategic nor conventional. As a weapon in the "grey-area" category, it would focus attention on the European theater as the site of potential East-West conflict. In his October speech, Schmidt had argued that any new arms control agreement would be seriously flawed if it did not try at some point to deal with a much wider range of weapons than envisaged at present: "SALT neutralized the strategic capabilities of the US and the Soviet Union in Europe, magnifying the significance of disparities between East and West as regards tactical nuclear and conventional weapons."[47]

A DISMAL DECEMBER

NATO consultation in December was again inconclusive. The arms control offers under consideration in Washington were not formally proposed, probably owing to interagency disagreement and rivalry. No firm commitments were made by either the United States or Europe. At a meeting of European defense ministers in a forum known as the "Eurogroup"—including representatives of the 15 NATO members, minus the United States, Canada, France, and Greece—reservations were expressed about the need for the weapons at all. As a result of the increasing efficiency of conventional antitank weapons—such as helicopter-carried missiles—European defense ministers requested a thorough review of all alternatives before deciding on the neutron warhead.[48] Yet reports from a meeting of defense ministers of 13 NATO nations, except France and Greece, in the Defense Planning Committee (DPC) the following day indicated that Britain, West Germany, and Belgium were "moving towards a decision to accept a small number of neutron warheads"[49] for the Lance missiles currently deployed with their forces in West Germany.

Neither the United States nor Europe conceded ground on the central issue—who would make the first commitment—but the United States did clarify its position. For the first time, Brown publicly admitted that "the decision . . . for development and production rests with the US President."[50] He reiterated the American concern that "we would not want a situation where we produced them and our allies decided they did not want them deployed."[51] He indicated that the issue of the first decision could be resolved by a private allied commitment to deployment in advance of an American announcement on production.

For Washington, the issue was no longer a question of *whether* the neutron bomb should be produced and deployed but rather a question of *how* the decision on production and deployment should be made. As such, it was a political, not a military, problem that required political skills rather than military analysis. After the NATO consultations in December, Brown had said that the neutron bomb had "become a political rather than a military problem,"[52] which was a matter "not for Ministers of Defense to decide but for Presidents to decide, and Chancellors."[53] As a political problem, the stakes on both sides of the Atlantic in the resolution of the controversy had increased. The ERW affair was now threatening the fabric of Alliance unity. The administration saw that a more forceful approach was needed to end the conflict. Higher–level officials and heads of governments would have to get involved.

Washington saw two reasons for making ERWs a higher priority in American policy. First, increased pressure by European governments on the United States to resolve the conflict was causing American credibility in Europe to decline dramatically. Carter and his administration were perceived as lacking political will and being unable to marshal domestic political resources in support of the defense of Western Europe. Europeans noted a lack of American political leadership in the inadequacy of Alliance consultation on the issue. In a sense, European leaders wanted Washington to impose order on their countries' divided opinions by announcing an unconditional decision to produce the weapons. Then European leaders could show their opponents that the United States, in fact, believed neutron weapons were essential to NATO's strategy of flexible response. Without such a demonstration of leadership, European politicians would be victimized by their opponents who viewed America's pluralist approach as a symbol of the declining American commitment to European defense.

The second reason for assigning a higher priority to ERWs was the intensification and effectiveness of the Soviet's propaganda campaign. During December the Soviet Union increased the frequency and scope of its condemnations of the neutron bomb. On December 12 *Tass* reported that "the broad campaign of protest launched in the USSR against US plans to create the neutron bomb is a vivid manifestation of the peaceful aspirations of Soviet people, of the policy of the CPSU [Communist Part of the Soviet Union] and the Soviet State aimed at improving the international climate."[54] Moscow did not limit its attacks to the United States, but also accused the Chinese of having plans to manufacture neutron weapons, drawing their inference from a poem by the deputy chief of staff of the Chinese People's Liberation Army.[55] Then, on December 23, Brezhnev proposed that Moscow and Washington jointly renounce production of the neutron bomb but indicated that the Soviet Union would produce its own version if the United States declined his offer. "If such a bomb were developed in the West, developed against us, a fact which nobody tries to conceal, the West must clearly realize that the USSR will not remain a passive onlooker," Brezhnev declared.[56]

In response, the administration embarked on deliberate campaign to defuse Soviet propagada. The neutron bomb was officially renamed the "Reduced Blast-Enhanced Radiation Warhead."[57] Administration officials sought to focus attention on the SS-20 to highlight Soviet weapons developments. Carter told journalists on December 30 that while the United States had deferred a decision on the neutron bomb, the Soviet Union had begun to deploy a "more destructive" and "destabilizing" weapon, the SS-20 mobile missile.[58] Brzezinski told reporters that the new Soviet missile was "more to be alarmed about" than the neutron weapon.[59] Efforts to counter Soviet criticism of the ERW had not been taken earlier because the Carter administration was seeking to project an image of support for arms control and disarmament. Moreover, active attention to Soviet criticism would be perceived as recognition that Soviet propaganda could influence Carter's decision. But time was running out, action had to be taken.

NOTES

1. Graham T. Allison, *Essence of Decision: Explaining the Cuban Missile Crisis* (Boston: Little, Brown, 1971), p. 178.

2. David Haworth, "US Says NATO Consensus is Needed on Neutron Bomb," *International Herald Tribune*, October 12, 1977.

3. During late 1977 and early 1978, a major European fear was that the United States might bargain away the much-coveted cruise missile in the SALT talks.

4. "Gromyko Calls for a UN Ban on the Neutron Bomb," *The Guardian* (London), September 28, 1977.

5. Interviews with U.S. government officials serving on the Special Coordinating Committee, Washington, D.C., August 1980.

6. Morton H. Halperin, *Bureaucratic Politics and Foreign Policy* (Washington, D.C.: The Brookings Institution, 1974), p. 109.

7. Rusk speaking to the policymaking officers of the Department of State, January 20, 1961, as quoted in Roger Hilsman, *To Move a Nation: The Politics of Foreign Policy in the Administration of John F. Kennedy*, (New York: Doubleday, 1967), p. 15.

8. Michael Getler, "No Bonn Bar Seen to Neutron Arms," Washington *Post*, September 28, 1977.

9. Ibid.

10. Ibid.

11. Ibid.

12. Dominick J. Coyle, "NATO Caution on Neutron Bomb," *Financial Times*, October 13, 1977.

13. "NATO Aides Fail to Agree on Neutron Bomb," *International Herald Tribune*, October 12, 1977.

14. Haworth, *International Herald Tribune*, October 12, 1977.

15. Bernard, Weinraub, "NATO Voices Concern Over Plans to Limit Cruise Missiles," New York *Times*, October 13, 1977, p. A9.

16. Dominick J. Coyle, "Italy Seeks Neutron Bomb Answers at NATO Talks," *Financial Times*, October 7, 1977.

17. Haworth, *International Herald Tribune*, October 12, 1977.

18. See Chapter 4.

19. Walter Pincus, "Victory Seen for US Neutron Arms Backers," Washington *Post*, November 24, 1977.

20. Interview with Robin Cook, Labour Member of Parliament, London, July 24, 1980.

21. David Buchan, "NATO and the Neutron Bomb," *Financial Times*, October 26, 1977.

22. Interview with Robin Cook.

23. Buchan, *Financial Times*, October 26, 1977.

24. Ibid.

25. Ibid.

26. Colonel Jonathan Alford, "The Neutron Bomb," *Command*, November/December 1978.

27. Interview with Richard Burt, Washington, D.C., August 20, 1980.

28. Ibid.

29. "NATO Aides Fail to Agree on Neutron Bomb," *International Herald Tribune*, October 13, 1977.

30. Buchan, *Financial Times*, October 26, 1977.

31. Arms Control Impact Statement for W-70 Mod. 3 (Lance) Warhead, in *Congressional Record*, July 13, 1977, p. S11764.

32. Term coined at the 1980 Millennium Conference, April 23-25 1980, London.

33.Robert G. Gray and Robert J. Bresler, "Why Weapons Make Poor Bargaining Chips," *Bulletin of Atomic Scientists*, September 1977.

34. Helmut Schmidt, "1977 Alastair Buchan Memorial Lecture," The International Institute for Strategic Studies, London, October 28, 1977, reprinted in *Survival* 20 (January/February 1978): 2-10.

35. Willy Brandt, "Dokumentation: Thesen zu Abrustung," *Die Neue Gesellschaft*, December 1977, p. 1001.

36. Richard Burt, "US May Offer Soviet Deal Shelving Neutron Bomb," New York *Times*, November 24, 1977.

37. Graf von Baudissin, "Hearing on the Enhanced Radiation Weapon," Evidence presented to the Standing Committee on Foreign Affairs and Defense, The Hague, November 7, 1977.

38. The use of bargaining chips in *arms control negotiations* was a common tactic in SALT I, but was a novel idea as applied to *weapons acquisition* in 1977-78. The so-called bargaining chip approach to SALT refers to the notion that weapons systems should be deployed less for their inherent strategic rationales than as bargaining chips to be traded in negotiations. U.S. Congress, Senate, Committee on Armed Services, *Hearings: Military Implications of the Treaty on the Limitation of Anti-Ballistic Missile Systems and the Interim Agreement on Limitation of Strategic Offensive Arms*, 92nd Cong., 2d sess., 1972, pp. 295, 369-70.

Henry Kissinger had urged research and development of strategic cruise missiles, partly so they might be used as SALT bargaining chips. Innovations in advanced weapons technology, such as MIRVs (multiple independent reentry vehicles) and cruise missiles, have often been used as bargaining chips with dual purposes. On the one hand,

they are justified as important tools of the negotiating process; on the other, they are used to quiet domestic opposition to arms control negotiations and make them more palatable to the defense community. But once a weapons system has been tested for deployment, the decision not to go into production cannot be taken without paying a high political price. Kissinger later lamented his bargaining chip approach to cruise missiles: "How was I to know the military would come to love it?" Raymond Garthoff, "SALT I: An Evaluation," *World Politics* 31 (October 1978).

Past experience with the bargaining chip approach indicates that weapons systems are negotiable only as long as they have not been produced and deployed. Once the production lines have been opened and new missions have been created, powerful alliances are created that object to the elimination of a new system in which the American taxpayer has already invested millions for research and development (R&D), testing, and production. One analyst recommended that "weapons which may be the subject of arms control negotiations and may serve as bargaining chips should be kept in R&D and away from the testing stage as long as is feasible." (Gray and Bresler). Thus in order to make the Soviets think that the United States was willing to "make a deal" on ERWs, it would have to give the appearance of being willing to forego deployment.

39. Quoted in *Congressional Record*, July 1, 1977, S11430.

40. Burt, New York *Times*, November 24, 1977.

41. Interview with Burt, August 20, 1980.

42. Burt, New York *Times*, November 24, 1977.

43. Pincus, Washington *Post*, November 24, 1977.

44. Ibid.

45. Harold Brown, "News Conference following the meeting of NATO's Defense Planning Committee at NATO Headquarters, Brussels," December 7, 1977, Selected Statements, January 1, 1978, p. 28.

46. Allison, p. 179.

47. Schmidt, *Survival*, January/February 1978.

48. "Some US Allies Voice Doubt on Neutron Arm," *International Herald Tribune*, December 6, 1977.

49. "European NATO Nations Indicate They May Ask for Neutron Bomb," New York *Times*, December 7, 1977, p. A3.

50. Brown, p. 27.

51. Ibid.

52. "Some US Allies Voice Doubt on Neutron Arm," *International Herald Tribune*, December 6, 1977.

53. Brown.

54. *Tass* in Russian for abroad, December 12, 1977, SBW, SU/5603/A1/1.

55. The poem, published in the *People's Daily*, read:

> The alloy steel is hard and solid no more,
> The neutron bomb is not difficult at all.
> With all talents delving into science and technology,
> We can scale the highest heights of the world.

quoted in "The Russians Fear New Chinese Bomb," *Sunday Observer* (London), December 18, 1977.

56. "Brezhnev Offer on the Neutron Bomb Accompanied by Threat," *Times* (London), December 24, 1977.

57. "US Army Steps Up Campaign to Boost Neutron Arms Image," *International Herald Tribune*, December 20, 1977.

58. Richard Burt, "US Seeks to Counter Neutron Bomb Criticism," New York *Times*, December 31, 1977, p. 3.

59. Ibid.

6

Political Fallout
from the Neutron Bomb

As the controversy over neutron weapons dragged on into 1978, now six months since Walter Pincus's article first appeared, doubts about Carter's ability to lead the process of nuclear decision making in the Alliance were translated into anxiety over the level of America's security commitment to Europe. Carter's personal commitment to disarmament and nonproliferation raised doubts in Europe about the president's resolve and ability to act decisively on matters of nuclear defense. The European concern about external security, however, was inextricably linked to domestic stability, especially in West Germany, where the Schmidt government was under pressure from its left-wing factions to reduce the country's dependence on weapons with improved warfighting capabilities. Carter's reservations over production and Schmidt's inhibitions over deployment created an impasse, with neither the United States nor its most important military ally willing to take the first step toward approving the weapon. For each government involved in the neutron bomb affair, the object was to find a solution most favorable to the political situation at home. But like the divergent interpretations of flexible response, the requirements of each government for domestic tranquillity were not always compatible.

MOSCOW'S MANEUVER

The level of tension between the allies increased in direct proportion to the intensity of Moscow's propaganda campaign. Washington officials tended to

believe that the stronger the criticism from Moscow, the more likely the allies were to endorse the weapon, in order to unify the Alliance against an external threat. But Soviet propaganda was fuel for European opponents of neutron weapons, especially for critics who sympathized with the Soviet Union. Moscow hoped to exploit allied disagreement by further inciting domestic opposition in Europe. Soviet leaders may have also thought they could dissuade West European governments from supporting the weapon by calling attention to prospects for continued détente between Eastern and Western Europe.

Moscow's major effort at dissuasion occurred when allied tensions over neutron weapons were in a state of flux. No agreement had been reached at the October meeting of the Nuclear Planning Group and domestic opposition continued to plague European governments. In mid-January Brezhnev sent personal letters to the heads of the principal West European governments warning them that deployment of the neutron bomb would jeopardize East-West détente.[1] Brezhnev claimed that deployment of the weapon would have adverse consequences on Europe's institutions of détente: the Conference on Security and Cooperation in Europe (CSCE) in Belgrade and the Mutual Balanced Force Reductions (MBFR) talks in Vienna.[2]

Yet in spite of its impact on opposition groups, Moscow's maneuver did not have the desired impact on European leaders. Brezhnev's letter seemed to increase the chances that the Alliance would decide to deploy neutron weapons. According to NATO sources, discussions among Alliance members on how to reply to the letter revealed indignation at the minatory tone of Brezhnev's missive and irritation at the implied assumption that NATO was obligated to justify its actions to the Warsaw Pact.[3] Some NATO officials suggested that Brezhnev had made it almost impossible for Europe not to endorse deployment because they would now appear to be knuckling under to Soviet pressure.[4] NATO members decided to emphasize a number of agreed points in their written replies to Brezhnev, although the precise emphasis was left to the discretion of individual governments. European leaders stressed that the development of neutron weapons was in large part a response to Soviet tank superiority in Europe, which, because of its financial constraints, could best offset this asymmetry by relatively cheap technological innovations like the ERW. The reply also argued that the neutron weapon is not, as Moscow contended, a weapon of mass destruction, but rather has less widespread radiation effects than NATO's current inventory of nuclear weapons and the Soviet Union's new armaments, among them the SS-20.[5]

European leaders adopted an equally minatory tone in their verbal rebuttals to Brezhnev. In a speech to the House of Commons on February 22, Prime Minister James Callaghan denounced the Soviet Union for using the neutron bomb issue as "propaganda cover" for its own weapons activities. If Moscow's objective was to prevent discussion of the development of its newest

innovation, the SS-20, Callaghan said, then Soviet leaders were harping on the wrong theme: Britain would not "succumb because of someone else's blackmail."[6] Washington welcomed Callaghan's statement against Moscow, although the prime minister had not offered a specific endorsement of the neutron weapon.

Brezhnev's letter also spurred much activity in West Germany. On February 21 the opposition CDU/CSU's parliamentary group passed a unanimous resolution in favor of deployment of neutron weapons.[7] The resolution stated that the weapon would augment NATO's deterrent power and added that the United States could not be expected to begin production unless Europe gave a clear signal in advance that the weapons could be deployed.[8] In an obvious attempt to weaken Schmidt's political image as a strong leader in the Western Alliance, Willi Weiskirch, an opposition defense spokesman, challenged Schmidt to take a "clear decision" on ERWs because Carter was waiting for an answer from his European allies.[9] A statement in favor of deployment was also expected from the SPD's coalition partner, the FDP, but pressure on Hans–Dietrich Genscher, the party's leader and minister of foreign affairs, by SPD members resulted in a compromised public position. The resolution adopted by the FDP was intended to satisfy both opponents and supporters of the weapons by stating that if the United States produced ERWs, two years would elapse before actual deployment, allowing time for NATO to undertake arms control negotiations with respect to the overall force posture in Europe.[10] In light of divided party opinion, the government's official stance remained equivocal. Bonn's official statement on February 23 said that it would seek to ensure that all possible progress toward arms control would be exploited in East-West negotiations before the neutron bomb was stationed in Europe: "The Federal Government's contribution to the NATO discussions will be guided by its vital interests and its responsibility in the field of defense and of maintaining the peace."[11] Claus Bolling, a government spokesman, stressed that the United States alone must decide to produce the weapon.[12] On the whole, the government appeared willing to acquiesce in deployment of the weapon if it could mollify left-wing opposition with a credible arms control offer and an unambiguous commitment from Washington.

THE ALLIANCE MOVES TOWARD AGREEMENT

By early 1978 the row over neutron weapons had grown to dimensions far larger than those initiated by the Pincus story. With the Alliance in visible disarray, the Soviet Union seemed to be enjoying a political heyday over its ability to upset NATO policies. One observer described the Soviet campaign against neutron weapons as the "most carefully orchestrated piece of arms control-by-public-relations since the same government's campaign against the

American ABM's in 1969."[13] The key to Soviet success was Moscow's ability "to take the disarmament initiative back from Mr. Carter and to reclaim a valued constituency it considers its own: those innumerable people to whom the threat of nuclear war is hateful."[14] This effect of Soviet criticism put Washington in an awkward position. Some American officials were concerned about the reception of Carter's disarmament, nonproliferation, and human rights policies abroad if Moscow could convincingly portray the president as a "war-monger" through the manipulation of this single, marginal weapon. Others were more worried that if the United States did not produce the weapon, its allies would draw the conclusion that the Soviets had forced the United States to succumb to their threats. "We can't let the world think that the Soviets can dictate our weapons policy," remarked one Washington observer.[15] Brown, Brzezinski, and Vance agreed that failure to go ahead with the weapon would cast doubt on American leadership within NATO.[16] The neutron bomb affair was rapidly becoming a test of NATO's ability to take difficult decisions in the face of overt Soviet pressure to prevent deployment.

With the scope of the conflict now encompassing much more than the weapon's purported military value, the neutron bomb became an increasingly important issue for the administration. As it became a higher priority in Washington, higher-ranking government officials became involved. The consequence was a marked deterioration in both intragovernmental and intra-Alliance communication. As responsibility was transferred to higher-ranking officials, the number of people involved, directly or otherwise, diminished. Many who had worked on the problem since June 1977 lost touch completely with the current issues and were assigned to other cases. Many who remained with the neutron bomb issue were unaware of the overall status of negotiations and were told only what they needed to know to perform their specific tasks. Information on most of the important issues was restricted to senior authorities. The consequence was a breakdown in the normal lines of communication between the United States and allied governments. According to State Department officials, the West German Embassy in Washington, whose communication with the State Department on important matters had been deteriorating since Carter had assumed office, was now relegated to an even more peripheral role on the neutron issue. Because high-level officials were worried about press leaks that might harm the delicate state of negotiations, they closed off all "nonessential" channels of communication. Too many people had been involved in the earlier stages, complicating the issues for the policymakers. Ambassadors were contacted but not consulted on the present state of negotiations. They became indignant about their lack of access and indirectly criticized the administration's high-level officials: "It is not so much that we are not talking at a high level, but that we are not talking very intelligently or profoundly," lamented one German official.[17]

In early 1978, the interagency team, now constituted at the assistant secretary level, decided that in order to resolve the crisis in alliance relations,

Washington had to intensify its political and diplomatic efforts; in the words of one State Department official, the United States would have to "force the issue within NATO forums." From January to March 1978 the State Department in particular worked aggressively to reach agreement with Bonn and London on a formula for a joint production and deployment decision. The new interagency team developed a strategy whose objective was to move toward deployment of ERWs through NATO consultation and bilateral negotiation. According to instructions from the NSC, supposedly reflecting the president's wishes, State Department officials put together a "package" of policy options that Washington hoped was flexible enough to get agreement from the principal allies. There was a general understanding among these officials that in order to make deployment politically feasible for the Europeans, a suitable arms control dimension would have to be included together with a decision to move ahead with production and deployment. American officials reasoned that European, especially West German, leaders would have a better chance of quieting their influential left-wing oppositions if the decision on deployment could be linked to an agreement to consider not deploying ERWs if a suitable arms control agreement could be reached within the two-year interim between production starts and actual deployment. American officials privately admitted, however, that they were not optimistic about the possibility of creating an arms control framework that would reflect an acceptable reduction in East and West armaments.

CONVOLUTED CONSULTATION

In an unpublicized meeting of NATO representatives on February 24, Leslie Gelb, the director of the State Department's Bureau of Politico-Military Affairs, unveiled a two-pronged strategy for achieving agreement on production and deployment. The proposal was based on the earlier interagency discussions about various arms control strategies, none of which had yet been formally presented to the allies. Option one called for bilateral U.S.-Soviet negotiations involving a direct trade-off between neutron weapons and the Soviet's SS-20. The second option was to introduce ERWs into the MBFR talks currently stalled in Vienna.[18] Both options were designed to defuse the Soviet propaganda campaign and ease European political constraints so that European leaders would find deployment acceptable. They had the additional advantage of seeming consistent with Carter's policies on disarmament and nonproliferation.

Since many U.S. officials expected the Soviet Union to reject both arms control offers,[19] they were not particularly concerned about the military impracticalities of either approach. On option one, defense analysts questioned the symmetry of negotiating the neutron bomb, a warhead for battlefield

artillery or short-range missiles, against the SS-20, an intermediate-range ballistic missile with three independently targetable warheads.[20] In the MBFR forum, there was again no comparable weapon that the Warsaw Pact countries could offer in exchange. As expected, Moscow rejected the suggestion that the United States might be able to use the neutron bomb as a bargaining chip to negotiate mutual restraint in the production of new types of weapons.[21] On March 11, the day after Harold Brown made public the suggestion of using neutron weapons as bargaining chips, the Soviet press agency, *Tass*, retorted in typical diplomatic fashion that "the Soviet Union again affirms its proposal and calls on the US for a mutual renunciation of the production of the neutron weapon."[22] Referring to the American proposal, *Tass* said that any attempt to link the weapon "with other questions that have no relation to it" would be unacceptable.[23]

From Washington's perspective, however, the proposals were directed not so much at Moscow as at Bonn, London, Brussels, and The Hague. Adoption of an arms control dimension by the United States was an expedient maneuver designed to provide political leverage for European leaders, particularly Schmidt, to rally their parties around a decision in favor of deployment. To achieve this objective it had to satisfy two conditions, of which actually limiting acquisition of neutron weapons was not one. First, the proposals would have to palliate public opposition to ERWs in Western Europe; at best they would assuage the fears of the vehemently opposed Dutch, Danes, and Norwegians; at least they had to subdue German and British criticism. For European opponents, making deployment dependent on a prior attempt at arms control could be interpreted as an effort to control weapons procurement if the Soviet Union exercised restraint. Second, the arms control offer had to stem the tide and influence of Soviet propaganda in Europe.

The European governments received Gelb's proposals with guarded optimism but still declined to offer a firm commitment. Whether the Europeans were prepared to commit themselves to deployment, even within an arms control framework, is still disputed today, depending on the perspective of the participant. State Department officials believe that Europe was receptive to Washington's plan and was preparing to make a public commitment at the next meeting of the North Atlantic Council (NAC), NATO's senior consultative body, on March 20. White House officials and some NSC staff members think that Schmidt hedged the issue until the very end, hoping that the United States would eventually make the first move.

The nature of the consultative process lends itself to these divergent interpretations. Alliance consultation is a fluid process: formal agreements and commitments are not made at every juncture, especially on the sensitive subject of nuclear weaponry. The very context of "allied" consultation may be a constraint in itself: governments do not want to display a measure of distrust by asking their allies for confirmation "in writing" of all tacit agreements.

Reticence on delicate issues is not uncommon. The formula for satisfying all allied participants was developed by building upon tacit agreements between the United States, the Federal Republic, and Britain. The first step was to establish the lowest common denominator of agreement. That the prolonged atmosphere of indecision within the alliance was instilling doubts among the allies was a likely starting point to which all concurred. It does not necessarily follow, however, that consensus existed on the best way of resolving the crisis of confidence. Explicit consent to every issue was not demanded; the United States assumed that the three governments implicitly agreed on the political necessity for deployment, at the very least. Alliance consultation, like common law, is built on compliance with unwritten rules and procedures. This makes consensus-building within NATO difficult to predict and describe. Precedent dictates acquiescence by NATO-Europe in American nuclear decisions, but excessive publicity and the novel approach of the Carter administration exercised a seemingly uncontrollable power on the direction of the neutron bomb debate.

The consultative process was also marred by a growing number of leaks. Shortly after the NATO meeting at which Gelb unveiled the arms control options, NATO officials who supported deployment intimated to European reporters that the United States was "preparing to announce its decision to produce ERWs for NATO deployment against Warsaw Pact tank armies in Europe."[24] This story was given credence by the testimony of General Alexander Haig, then commander of NATO, to the Senate Armed Services Committee, to the effect that most of Europe's military leaders favored deployment of the neutron bomb.[25] These allegations incensed opponents of the weapon and damaged allied attempts at "quiet diplomacy."

THE DUTCH DECLINE

Whatever agreements were being worked out in private consultation within NATO were jolted by a series of tumultuous events in the Netherlands, culminating in the resignation of the Dutch defense minister in protest over the government's policy on neutron weapons. Following the government's pronouncement on February 23 to yield to parliamentary pressure and try to prevent the deployment of ERWs in Europe, the lower house of Parliament reversed its position and defeated two antineutron bomb motions on March 1.[26] One of these motions, by the ruling Christian Democrats, would have prevented the addition of ERWs to NATO's nuclear arsenal but would have allowed them to be used as a bargaining chip in arms control negotiations.[27] Defense Minister Roelof Krusanga, a Christian Democrat, had urged the government to adopt this approach in debate in Parliament a week earlier, surprising MPs with his assessment that the government would oppose the

weapon. Only minutes before this statement, Dr. Christoph van der Klaauw, foreign minister and a member of the right-wing Liberal Party, had advised Parliament not to close off its options before discussions with NATO partners.[28] The governing Christian Democratic-Liberal coalition, only three months old, appeared unable to reconcile its differences. Then on March 5 Dr. Krusanga, a vigorous opponent of ERW deployment, resigned his portfolio when other cabinet members refused to denounce the weapon.[29] The Liberals were pushing for at least a neutral position on deployment, but their governing partner was by and large opposed to the weapon and was under strong pressure by the Council of Churches to heed their humanitarian arguments against the introduction of the weapons in Europe.[30] In a speech to Parliament three days later, Premier Andreas van Agt turned the issue over to the legislators. He promised not to give Washington a commitment to deploy the weapons prior to East-West talks to limit their introduction.[31] But he told opponents of the weapon that Parliament would make the final decision on whether the neutron bomb would be deployed with the Dutch forces committed to NATO.[32] On the same day the Dutch Parliament, by a vote of 110-40, adopted a resolution "opposing production of the neutron and calling on the government to notify the US and other allies in the North Atlantic Treaty Organization of its action."[33] As the Dutch were now firmly committed not to deploy neutron weapons, the number of European allies willing to join West Germany in stockpiling the weapons had diminished. Moreover, the vehemence with which the public was opposing the weapon was bound to fuel public resistance in other NATO countries and add grist to Moscow's propaganda mill.

THE ILL-FATED NAC

By mid-March 1978 most American officials believed they had reached a clear understanding with the allies of the need to deploy the neutron bomb. They expected to announce a joint production and deployment decision at the March 20 NAC (pronounced "nack") meeting. Although Schmidt had seemed to vacillate on his commitment to the American plan, by March the State Department was convinced that the chancellor was "on board." The formula for deployment worked out in private negotiations with the allies had three stages:

1. Carter would authorize production of the weapons.
2. Washington would offer to bargain with the Soviet Union about limiting deployment.
3. NATO would move ahead with deployment if East-West talks failed to produce mutually agreeable limitations.[34]

The United States preferred to bargain with the Soviets on the SS-20, a weapon that it believed threatened the overall strategic balance; however, Washington was prepared to leave that issue vague in the final agreement with the allies because some Europeans preferred to seek a trade-off at MBFR.

Final preparations for the NAC were based on the assumption of American officials that the conditions for ERW deployment in Europe had been worked out carefully enough in Bonn, London, and Washington that public agreement was a reasonable expectation. Most of official Washington believed it had created a scenario that would be "livable for all." State Department negotiators worked with their British and West German counterparts through mid-March putting the finishing touches on a formula for deployment that the three governments would find politically acceptable. According to one American participant, the negotiations went as far as providing "a footnote for the Dutch," in order to avoid a veto. In addition, the three negotiating teams had worked out a formula for tacit acceptance by Italy, Denmark, and Norway, all of which were ardently opposed to deployment. Under the compromise plan, the United States would begin producing neutron weapons, but their deployment would be held up for 18 to 24 months while the Alliance tested Moscow's reaction to the idea of limiting the neutron bomb in return for restrictions on the Soviet's new SS-20. If the arms control attempt failed, Alliance members would allow the United States to begin deploying neutron weapons in Europe.[35] Included in the plan was a statement that the production decision was purely American.[36] Most participants were satisfied with the compromise: "The Europeans were as, forthcoming as you could possibly expect of them," said one U.S. participant.[37] According to a State Department official, both the State and Defense Departments had "done the necessary spade work to get the allies to agree. By this time, the allies were no longer a problem."

This attitude is consistent with the expectations of State Department officials: Having expended much diplomatic time and effort to "bring the allies on board," they would be inclined to believe in the potential success of their efforts. Some NSC members, however, were still skeptical about the Germans' willingness to agree to deployment. At one point, Brzezinski turned a framed, autographed photograph of Schmidt to face the wall in his office as a sign of his annoyance with the chancellor. One NSC member argued that the United States had reason to doubt, right up to March 20, the assurances by Bonn and London that an agreement could be concluded at the NAC meeting.[38]

Suddenly all the plans were overturned. During the weekend of March 18-19, Carter telephoned Brzezinski from Georgia, where he was spending a weekend fishing, to tell him that he had looked over the decision memoranda submitted by the interagency task force and decided to cancel the Brussels meeting and scrap the compromise agreement. Many in the State Department's Bureau of Politico-Military Affairs were spending the weekend at the office,

drafting final diplomatic instructions for the NAC meeting on Monday. On Sunday evening, Brzezinski phoned the State Department to inform them of Carter's decision not to go ahead with production and deployment. The announcement struck like a thunderbolt, sending a shock wave through all those who had spent most of their working hours over the last few months trying to achieve an alliance-wide consensus and leaving some people "literally laying on the floor." A cable was quickly sent to Brussels postponing the meeting.

By every indication thus far, no one would have predicted Carter's abrupt reversal. Even the secretaries of state and defense and the national security advisor were overwhelmed. Although the president's intentions could not be definitively ascertained before the announcement of his final decision, all U.S. government agencies were operating under the assumption that Carter was fully aware of their efforts to convince the allies to permit deployment. Theoretically, Carter could (and did) play the card of cancellation, but in reality the constraints imposed by the intensification of Washington's political strategy for obtaining an allied consensus implicitly limited the feasibility of rejecting the weapon so late in the game. In games of strategy alternative options are often reserved for unpredictable contingencies; however, in the ERW case, it is clear that the option of cancellation had not been protected for the president throughout the months of difficult negotiation. Although a deferral option was not deliberately closed off, the risks of deferral increased manifold as Washington increased pressure on the allies to permit deployment. Moreover, American officials, on balance, seemed convinced that deployment was the preferable option.

CARTER'S FISHING TRIP

What then prompted Carter to reverse his administration's course of action at the eleventh hour, when the Alliance seemed so close to agreement? It is important to note that the final outcome of the neutron bomb controversy was the result of two decisions: first, to scrap the compromise arrangement worked out by the president's senior advisors with their British and German counterparts; second, to "defer production of weapons with enhanced radiation effects," making the ultimate decision dependent on "the degree to which the Soviet Union shows restraint in its conventional and nuclear arms programs and force deployments."[39] The first decision was made by Carter in isolation over the weekend of March 18-19; the second was a compromise solution adopted by the President on April 6, at the urging of his advisors and pressure from Congress.

After a grueling week in Washington in which Carter pushed the Senate to approve the Panama Canal treaties, the president flew to Georgia for a

weekend of fishing. Included in his weekend homework was a decision memorandum from Vance and Brown, drafted by their deputies, Leslie Gelb and David McGiffert, respectively. The memo outlined the phases of the compromise arrangement with the allies. According to one of the authors of the memo, the alternatives were presented in such a way as to leave no doubt that these officials favored approval of the plan. Carter was to make his decision known by checking one of two boxes: proceed or cancel.

Looking over the memo, Carter is said to have been shocked to find that NATO was on the verge of approving the compromise plan.[40] One Carter aide later remarked that "it was clear to everybody that the President was angry" when he learned how far things had gone.[41] Another aide commented that "the bureaucracy had proceeded on his inclination to produce the neutron bomb with less concern for the conditions he wanted met."[42] He later explained to his aides that the condition he wanted met in any arrangement with the allies was a "unilateral public commitment" by Chancellor Schmidt to deploy neutron weapons if the United States should proceed with production.[43] An administration official later tried to explain the motives behind Carter's insistence on this condition:

> He was concerned about his image and did not want to be viewed as a big weapons man. His feeling was that in the past 30 years the President of the United States had to take a great deal of political heat on important military decisions and this time he did not want to take it alone, especially with full-fledged, economically powerful allies.[44]

But his advisors in the State and Defense Departments have privately asserted that they were never given specific instructions from the president on such conditions. Apparently compliance with this condition was tacitly assumed by Carter in his formulation of the steps necessary to resolve the crisis to his satisfaction. But even the president later admitted to an aide: "I should have made sure I knew where we were going on this earlier."[45] Poor communication with his aides and reticence in expressing his specific objectives had created a gap between Carter's goals and those of his administration.

Most of the administration thought the goal was production and deployment of neutron weapons, based on the assessment that the costs to Alliance relations of not proceeding would be greater than the potential damage to ongoing arms control negotiations if the Alliance did go ahead. It was a choice between the lesser of two evils; no one would "win" on this issue. The resolution depended on minimizing losses. But the president is likely to have given more weight to other factors; elements that formed the foundation of his foreign policy goals based on his firm conviction that "US dependence on nuclear power should be kept to a minimum" and that force is not the most useful tool in diplomacy.[46] At the same time, Carter was torn between his

moral convictions and political pragmatism. A principal factor in Carter's own analysis of the pros and cons of the neutron weapon is likely to have been a fundamental ambivalence about the issues. Recall that at the outset of the controversy in summer 1977, Carter had asked Congress to approve funds for the weapon so that he could "keep his options open." He wanted leeway on the matter precisely because he himself was uncertain about the weapon's merits. In his remarks he had presented issues on both sides of the debate. As a former nuclear engineer, Carter was apt to scrutinize the technical features or weapons characteristics of the warhead. On this matter, there are no definitive answers. As mentioned before, the ERW might be marginally beneficial or detrimental to deterrence and defense; it would neither decisively augment nor detract from NATO's force posture. As Carter was prone to drawn-out, protracted deliberations and tended to delve into the minutiae of decisions, his personal analysis may have increased his ambivalence.

Not only was his technical analysis of neutron weapons marred by ambivalence, but Carter's assessment of the political implications of the decision was also subject to ambiguity. Any rational type of analysis he may have used to arrive at a decision was limited by the amount and quality of information he had before him at the time. Information here refers to both knowledge about the specific issues and events communicated to the president by his aides and his personally acquired knowledge or understanding of Alliance procedures and domestic politics in Europe. According to inside sources, Carter may not have been continuously and completely informed on the issues by his staff because none of his aides on the NSC were strong "Europeanists."[47] The staff may have tended to minimize the importance of European sensitivity to the weapon in its communication with the president. Several Europeans had expressed dissatisfaction with their dealings with the Carter administration. American officials were described as "provincial" or "unable to speak with Europeans." One European said: "They just don't understand us."[48] In addition, the president's top aides may not have had a meaningful sense of his qualms about ERWs because Carter had a penchant for keeping his personal dilemmas to himself. Some officials have accused Vance, Brown, and Brzezinski of not briefing the president with sufficient clarity on the momentum of the political efforts being pressed on the Europeans. Incremental steps and achievements were not organized into cohesive memoranda for the president. Each independent action or initiative means little unless it is viewed within a comprehensive and coherent framework. Such a situation resulted both from the formal nature of discussions about neutron weapons with the administration once it had become a national and international controversy and the informal planning among organizations. As the matter increased in sensitivity and the flow of information to officials became limited and fragmented, it is likely that the president's aides themselves were sometimes so confused as to the overall political strategy that they felt

unable to present their chief with a concise overview of the situation. Most importantly, though, Carter's closest aides probably sensed the president's ambivalence about the weapon, and thus felt that if they waited until an agreement was imminent, then their case for going ahead with the arrangement would be all the more credible. If the president was indeed an "uncommitted thinker," and therefore open to suggestion, perhaps limiting the flow of unpleasant information about the Europeans' reservations during the early stages of conflict would help to persuade the president of the finality of the compromise agreement.

Carter's ability to make a fully informed decision was also constrained by his limited knowledge of Alliance procedures and of European domestic politics. He seems to have failed to grasp the significance of his radical approach to Alliance decision making in asking the allies to come forth with a commitment on deployment prior to his decision on production. His move away from the unilateral responsibilities of the United States to a pluralist model of Alliance decision making was taken implicitly without conscious reflection on the implications of altering the accepted procedure. But Europe's impression of this stylistic change was bewilderment at the slew of contradictory statements emanating from Washington and dismay at the president's seeming inability to run the government: "President Carter doesn't like to impose authority and set a position," one NATO official commented. "He seems to think this public debate is healthy."[49] The New York *Times* noted that

> the president may well underestimate just how much he has strained relations with West Germany. Ever since he took office Washington has seemed to nag at Bonn—over its proposed sale of a nuclear reprocessing plant to Brazil, over its alleged failure to contribute enough to reinvigorating the Western economy, over Western strategies for dealing with the Soviet Union and over the neutron warhead, too. The German decision to go forward with deploying the weapon was not taken lightly.[50]

In Carter's view, however, he was perhaps perceptively responding to Europe's long-standing criticism of Washington's overbearing leadership in NATO. This perspective led him to interpret European reservations on deployment as a sign of unwillingness rather than a signal that Carter should go ahead and they would then follow his lead. Misperception on both sides of the Atlantic led Carter to believe that he would be "crawling out on a limb" by "letting the Germans decide"[51] whether to deploy the weapon. On the other hand, Schmidt believed that he had personally gone out on a limb by preparing to permit deployment before receiving a firm commitment from Carter on production.

All these factors—poor communication, lack of information, and misperception of the allies—seem to have increased Carter's ambivalence to the

point where he could be shocked by the extent of agreement between the United States and the allies. He was overwhelmed by the tenuousness of Schmidt's commitment despite his advisors' assertions to the contrary. The risk of being "caught out on a limb" if Schmidt then refused to deploy the weapons seemed too great. Carter's ambivalence also made him vulnerable to the opinions of informal advisors, especially given the poor communication with his official advisors. A number of senior administration officials have suggested that Carter was influenced by the arguments against the neutron bomb offered by Andrew Young, a close friend of the president, about the time of Carter's fishing trip. Young, the chief U.S. representative at the United Nations, argued that moving ahead with the ERW would expose the United States to fierce criticism by the international community. At the UN Special Session on Disarmament, to be held in New York on May 23, the neutron bomb would dwarf Carter's efforts to limit the spread of nuclear weapons, Young claimed.[52] As Carter was not wholly convinced of the military merits of the weapon, he did not want to bear the entire political burden for what could be an "ugly" decision. No, it was safer to cancel the March 20 meeting, scrap the compromise agreement, and bury the whole matter. In a state of ambivalence, Carter seems to have let personal convictions and momentary pressures be his guide. Despite his attempt to bring the allies into the decision-making process, Carter made his decision without the allies' help. As the New York *Times* commented:

> The best explanation may be that Mr. Carter has never reconciled himself to the cumbersome policy process. He may regard decisions as still open when others see them as closed. . . . Mr. Carter may never have grasped just how much momentum he had, perhaps unwittingly, imparted to the project and how difficult it now is to turn that momentum aside.[53]

The way that Carter arrived at his decision raises a question that has not yet been satisfactorily answered: Why was the president not briefed on the necessary details of the State Department's negotiations with the allies? To many in the State Department, the lack of coordination between the president and his staff is still a mystery. The ERW case does not reflect the development of a well-organized interagency mechanism for policy formulation and implementation. One participant lamented: "No overall strategy, in fact, ever existed." The approach took the shape of "lurching through every day, trying to stay on top of the issue, but never knowing for sure if a positive finale was possible." For most officials involved, the neutron bomb quickly acquired the status of an untouchable or undesirable issue because all believed that the final outcome would not make any of them look good in the eyes of their superiors. Because the ERW case was identified very early as a "no-win event," no U.S. official or agency wanted to accept the blame for the poorly devised and executed political strategy; therefore, they psychologically brushed it aside as

either a "non-issue" or a problem for which they were not responsible. Seen in a bureaucratic politics framework, each player was trying to protect his position and professional interests.

But in trying to keep their slates clean, some of Carter's aides may have committed one of the greatest blunders of the ERW fiasco through an act of omission, namely, not adequately informing the bureaucracy of the president's views.[54] Yet the same officials also claim that an equally grave error may have been committed by Carter because his indecisiveness and vacillation kept him from giving his NSC staff clear instructions for implementing his objectives. The NSC's principal role is that of coordinator of foreign and national security policy, not of sole formulator of the president's policies. One participant outlined the three stages of policy coordination between the president and the NSC. First, the president is presented with the issues and debates from which goals and objectives are formulated. Second, the president is presented with a full range of alternative options from which to make his decision. Finally, after the president has weighed the consequences of each alternative, he makes his decision, which is then implemented by the NSC. If the NSC did not adequately fulfill the requirements of the first two stages, the policymaking role would, by default, fall to the NSC. Some officials claim that "there is no evidence that the NSC worked closely with Carter during the nine-month affair; if anything, Carter seems to have been unusually uninformed." Another participant claimed that several NSC members were "competing for a piece of the action," suggesting that the personal rivalry within the NSC may have prevented the president from receiving complete and relatively unbiased information. According to another official, the bureaucrats responsible for coordinating policy on the neutron bomb tended to give higher priority to information received from NATO headquarters in Brussels than to messages relayed from Bonn. While they reflect the views of their governments, members of NATO's military staffs tend to put more emphasis on the military balance than do some politicians in the national capitals.[55] Thus communication from NATO headquarters was usually phrased in more positive tones than similar material from Bonn. Simply by attributing a slightly different emphasis to the wording of messages and cables and by manipulating the "key-word" distribution system used in interagency communication, the dissemination of vital information to key decision makers could be blocked. One participant asserted that "the political dictates of the Bureaucracy fouled the decision-making process on ERWs." Even an NSC official directly involved in the controversy admits that Washington's management of the political process "could have been better." "If there is a lesson in all of this, it must be about communications," said another official, "Either nobody told the President that the Alliance was moving ahead with the neutron bomb or he didn't care to listen."[56]

TRANSATLANTIC COMMUNICATION GAP

After Brzezinski told State Department officials to terminate efforts to achieve an allied consensus on neutron weapons, the State Department cabled Brussels with a message that procedural difficulties had made it necessary to postpone the March 20 meeting. The allies may have been a bit confused, but they as yet had no reason to suspect any change of plans. According to one British participant, the cancellation of the meeting was not interpreted as a signal of an imminent overthrow of the previous course. In fact, the allies may have been reassured that the agreement would come to fruition by General Haig's remarks the following day, March 21. As Commander of U.S. forces in Europe, Europeans could assume that Haig was speaking with the president's authority. While admitting that the neutron warhead was a "very sensitive political question," Haig asserted that "it is a most desirable modernization step to be taken by the Alliance."[57]

Meanwhile in Washington, Vance, Brown, and Brzezinski were as stunned as their subordinates at Carter's eleventh-hour reversal. At a meeting on March 20 these three top foreign policy officials discussed the new assessment with President Carter, Vice-President Mondale, and chief White House aide Hamilton Jordan. Vance and Brown intervened directly to try to persuade the president that at this stage in allied consultation, and after a relatively successful propaganda campaign by the Soviets, he simply could not cancel the weapon outright. The allies would be left empty-handed, Moscow would claim a victory over its imperialist foes, and the Untied States would be blamed for a lack of credibility and leadership. Carter is said to have expressed doubts about Schmidt's willingness to allow deployment and to have informed his aides that without a unilateral public commitment by the chancellor he would not approve production.[58] Carter disagreed with his advisors, but conveyed a sense of ambiguity that led his advisors to believe they could "come back and argue again."[59] Top foreign policy officials were convinced that outright cancellation would damage the administration's leadership within NATO as well as raise doubts about Washington's credibility elsewhere. To obtain public support for their views and reassure Western leaders, some administration officials told a reporter on March 27 that "NATO would soon agree to a plan that could enable the United States to begin producing the controversial neutron bomb later this year."[60]

Carter, again in a state of indecision after meeting with his advisors, owed a personal explanation to Schmidt and Callaghan. A week had passed since the cancellation of the March 20 NATO meeting, and every newspaper in Europe seemed to carry a slightly different version of what was going on in Washington.[61] Deputy Secretary of State Warren Christopher was dispatched to West Germany and Britain with oral instructions from the president to explain that the United States could not go ahead with production without a

commitment on deployment from Europe. Christopher had been instructed to say that the president's judgment was not yet final and to seek European reaction.[62] Carter may have questioned his original judgment on Europe's hesitancy in light of his advisors' arguments to the contrary, and thought that Schmidt would either now come forth with a firm public commitment or confirm the president's first assessment by expressing satisfaction with cancellation. What the president wanted, commented one aide, was to "smoke 'em out, bring things to a head and see where they stand. . . . There's no reason to produce a weapon if our allies won't even say they want it."[63] After Christopher received oral instructions at the White House on March 27, one of Carter's aides asked that the State Department's Bureau of Politico-Military Affairs draft a memo setting forth background "talking points" for his confrontation with Schmidt.[64] The memo was to be cabled to the U.S. Embassy in Bonn, where Christopher planned to arrive on March 30 to see Foreign Minister Hans-Dietrich Genscher. But the author of the memo either misunderstood his instructions or, more likely, deliberately drafted a cable that was described as "a lot sharper and starker" than Carter's instructions to Christopher.[65] It gave the impression that the president had made a final decision against the neutron bomb. When Christopher read the cable in Bonn he realized that it exceeded Carter's oral instructions. In his conversation with Genscher in Bonn on March 30 and with Schmidt in Hamburg the following day, Christopher stuck to his oral instructions and advised them only that Carter was "leaning against" production because of a "lack of a united policy in NATO," implying that Europe might yet be able to salvage the situation.[66] Nevertheless, Schmidt and Genscher were flabbergasted by the news. Schmidt even asked Christopher to phone Washington to check that his instructions were correct. After confirmation that they were indeed correct, Schmidt called an emergency meeting of his closest advisors. He then told Christopher that he was prepared to support Carter if the production decision was made. He also asked that a decision to cancel production of the weapons be announced as Carter's own, without blaming NATO governments for lack of support. Schmidt requested that the president postpone a formal announcement of his decision until Foreign Minister Genscher had spoken with Carter personally so that it would be publicly clear that the West Germans supported production.

Bonn had its own domestic political concerns: It was apparently worried that some members of the Carter administration might seek to depict the Schmidt government as an "appeaser or scapegoat" whose alleged reluctance to deploy the weapons could be used to explain a decision by President Carter not to go ahead with production.[67] The Social Democratic government was also concerned that the right-wing Christian Democratic opposition would accuse Schmidt of having resisted a weapons system that could have increased West Germany security[68] and as having little influence within the U.S. administration over an issue of vital importance to national security.

Christopher agreed that the Alliance should try to salvage whatever unity was left in this affair, and Genscher's visit to Washington was moved up two days to April 4. Nevertheless, Bonn was infuriated; as *Time* Diplomatic Correspondent Strobe Talbott observed, "Christopher's mission to Bonn was a risky way for one ally to deal with another, and particularly for Washington to deal with Bonn. Given all the tensions of the last year, the Germans were sure to look on the tactic as diplomatic blackmail."[69]

THE PERSISTENCE OF THE PRESS

With both the Alliance and the Carter administration now in visible disarray, a number of pressures converged to force the president to alter the final form of his decision not to proceed with neutron weapons. Having adopted a pluralist approach to Alliance decision making, the president was subject to all the influences of various groups who sought to make use of the confusion for their own purposes. The pressures were exerted by the press, the allies, Congress, and, of course, Carter's foreign policy advisors. The purposes of each were different, but they demonstrated the difficulties of trying to make nuclear decisions by consensus without a clear sense of the outcome desired.

As the press had been the catalyst for the controversy in June 1977, now it again helped to shape the final outcome of the nine-month fiasco. After giving Christopher oral instructions on March 27 for his meetings with Schmidt, Genscher, and British Foreign Secretry David Owen,[70] Carter left Washington for a seven-day tour of South America and Africa. In the meantime, Richard Burt, then a reporter for the New York *Times*, got hold of the State Department's cable to Christopher.[71] The cable read: "The President has reached a judgment not to produce the enhanced radiation warhead."[72] Though the cable began with a clear warning that its language had not been cleared by the president or the secretary of state, it was nevertheless an official administration document. One administration aide said the leak "either came from someone who was trying to force us into a certain decision or from someone who was trying to hurt us in the Senate on SALT."[73] Burt received the information on Monday night, April 3, as Carter was flying in from Africa, and on Tuesday the front-page headline read: "Aides Report Carter Bans Neutron Bomb; Some Seek Reversal, Arms Goals are Cited."[74] The story threw Carter and most of his top advisors into a rage. Brzezinski, Brown, and Vance wanted to draft the final decision in as politically palatable a manner as possible. Now the chances appeared even slimmer than before. At an emergency meeting of the president and his chief foreign policy advisors at the White House on April 4, discussion centered on how to react to Burt's story. The president wanted to deny its contents completely, but Secretary of Energy James Schlesinger pointed out that the story had already been conclusively

confirmed by sources at the New York *Times*.[75] Vance, Brzezinski, and Brown were all concerned, sometimes for conflicting reasons, about the impact of the move on the allies, on sensitive negotiations with the Soviet Union, and on Carter's relations with Congress.[76] What signals would be sent by such a decision? It would tell the NATO allies that Carter was unpredictable and perhaps willing to sacrifice Alliance concerns for progress on U.S.-Soviet bilateral issues. It would tell Moscow that, given enough pressure, the president might well back down on controversial weapons decisions and was clearly so anxious to get a summit and a SALT II treaty that Moscow need not make any more concessions. It would tell the Senate, which already doubted Carter's ability to conclude a satisfactory SALT treaty, that the president could not be trusted to take the kind of tough stands necessary to preserve the power balance with the Soviet Union and that senators ought to give the treaty an even more skeptical review. Few, including those who strongly supported a new SALT agreement, believed that a decision to cancel the weapon would result in more accommodating policies by the Soviet Union.[77]

To "clear the air for a few days," Secretary Vance responded to Burt's article with an announcement that "no decision has been made"[78] but would be announced "very soon."[79] But the administration's efforts to deny the New York *Times* report proved ineffective. Complained a top presidential aide: "I suppose it's in the nature of the presidency that we have to take responsibility for an inaccurate leak."[80] Even Secretary of Defense Brown conceded that "it's obvious from the nature of the press coverage that we could have handled it better."[81] Carter's national security advisors were now pushing wholeheartedly for a decision that would not definitively cancel the weapon, despite any personal misgivings they had about its military effectiveness. Privately, however, the president's chief advisors thought he would stick to his original decision to cancel the weapon entirely.[82] "The real fight for that week—Tuesday April 4 to April 7—was to work out a formula by which the weapon could in essence be canceled, and by which political damage could be limited through deferral."[83] The options considered at this point were to cancel the weapon entirely or to halt production but leave open the possibility of going ahead at some later date.[84] Administration officials assumed that the second option was strongly preferred by West German leaders.[85] But while a decision to postpone a complete ban on neutron weapons production might reduce friction with West Germany and other NATO members, it would also create other problems. In particular, officials contended that it would not dampen Moscow's criticism of the weapons and would not end the growing debate on Capital Hill.[86] Accordingly Hamilton Jordan, the president's assistant, and Jody Powell, his press secretary, were said to believe that Carter should not budge from his earlier decision,[87] contrary to the advice of Brown, Brzezinski, and Vance. Washington seemed to be the site of "a battle between contending factions around the President."[88]

BONN AND WASHINGTON

In the midst of this bureaucratic infighting and presidential uncertainty, Foreign Minister Hans-Dietrich Genscher arrived in Washington to discuss the status of the neutron bomb. Before leaving Bonn, Genscher told leaders of German political parties in strict confidence that he would press Carter to produce the weapon "in unilateral action" without waiting for European agreement.[89] Genscher's concern that Carter likely would decide not to produce the weapon reflected concern for its impact on his government's political stature at home more than a fear that West Germany's security would be endangered. As Richard Neustadt has noted, alliance politics consist of the "interaction of intragovernmental games."[90] Schmidt's stakes arose from Bonn politics; Carter's from Washington politics. The weapon itself was merely the conduit for conflict. Bonn was nervous about possible effects the decision would have on the West German political situation. Schmidt worried that, although he felt he had expressed his willingness to deploy the weapons to Carter, and despite opposition from his party's left–wing, members of the Carter administration would try to portray the chancellor as a chameleon responsible for the cancellation of the program.[91] Such a portrayal by Washington would allow the CDU/CSU to accuse the Schmidt government of appeasing the Soviet Union and thus deal the SPD a political setback in a year in which four important state elections were scheduled.[92] So in Bonn's opinion, Genscher was making every possible effort to tailor his position to Carter's satisfaction.

Genscher thought he lobbied hard with Carter, Vance, Brown, and Brzezinski against scrapping the weapons, assuring them that Bonn really did back their deployment on German soil. Stationing the weapon in Europe, he said, should, as a first step, be made a major issue in arms control negotiations between the United State an the USSR.[93] This was a major concession for the Schmidt government, which had preferred to bargain for a reduction in existing Soviet tanks rather than for a limitation on as yet undeployed Soviet missiles. Genscher promised, if no concessions were made in return by the Soviets, that Europe would add the weapon to its nuclear arsenal.[94] He even said publicy: "We feel that this should be produced."[95] To Genscher, this looked like the endorsement Washington had been seeking for months.

But Carter seems to have interpreted the foreign minister's remarks differently. In his response, Carter reproached Genscher for Bonn's scant public enthusiasm.[96] He was still unwilling to make the unilateral decision to produce the weapons without Germany's prior public agreement to deploy them. In Carter's opinion, Bonn did not understand the stakes in the president's political game: without being able to cite Europe's unconditional commitment to deployment, he would be seen as contradicting his commitments to disarmament and nonproliferation. From his perspective, Bonn's support was still insufficient. Carter interpreted Genscher's statement that the weapon

"should be produced" as a circumvention of the issue of deployment. That Bonn wanted Washington to bear the entire burden was reinforced in Carter's eyes by Genscher's statement that "We [Bonn] made our position clear long ago and said we think the decision to produce is an American decision."[97] To make Carter more uncomfortable, Genscher is said to have asked "some embarassing questions" about Carter's last-minute reversal.[98] In a final effort to see whether West Germany would come out publicly for deploying the weapon, Genscher was apparently asked if the fact that Britain was ready to do so might change Bonn's position.[99] Genscher is said to have told American officials that if another continental ally, such as Belgium, would call for deployment, Bonn might reconsider,[100] but Britain alone was insufficient. And although he asked Carter to keep open the possibility of eventual deployment, Genscher told reporters that "this is not a German–American issue," it involves "all the allies."[101] "At that point" an American official recalled, "we knew that the Germans were never going to give the president the help he needed and that there was no other alternative but to stop production."[102] The help Carter needed was to avoid being seen as responsible for introducing the neutron bomb into NATO.

But while Carter remained determined not to order production, pressure from Congress and elsewhere in support of the weapon led him to adopt a course that would halt immediate plans for deployment, but would allow the Pentagon to continue its modernization program, without requiring a decision on neutron warheads.

CONGRESS COMPLAINS

Congress was the next group to open fire on the president. Its criticism was important not only for its impact on the final version of Carter's neutron bomb decision but also because it would add weight to the arguments of senators who felt the administration was "negotiating from weakness"[103] on SALT. The politics of the neutron bomb controversy cannot be understood apart from other vital issues, such as SALT. Congressmen who had been persuaded not to scrap the weapon at the outset were shocked to read of its cancellation in the newspapers. Senate Majority Leader Robert Byrd called the president to reaffirm his support for the weapon[104] and to warn of the diminished chance of Senate ratification of SALT II if Carter canceled the neutron bomb without a Soviet *quid pro quo*. "This could be seen as surrendering to the Russians' massive propaganda campaign," Byrd told Carter; "and that would encourage the Soviets to think we would be intimidated on other matters,"[105] an obvious reference to SALT. Senator Charles Percy said that Carter "would be making a major mistake if he decides unilaterally not to produce and deploy the neutron bomb."[106] He added that the weapon "could be enormously effective as a

bargaining chip in arms negotiations with the Soviet Union."[107] In a three-page statement, Senator Sam Nunn, a member of the Armed Services Committee, warned that a decision to halt the weapon "risks torpedoing" efforts to improve European defenses and "would place in the minds of the Soviets the image of a timid and hesitant American Government which lacks the courage to confront the difficult defense choices ahead."[108] Some senators who opposed SALT would probably have welcomed a public showdown on the neutron bomb because the reaction in NATO would have made it more difficult for the administration to win ratification of a new SALT treaty.

The House of Representatives did not remain silent either. The Democratic chairman of the House Armed Services Committee, Melvin Price, joined the committee's ranking Republican, Bob Wilson, in a letter to the president arguing against any decision to stop production of the weapon.[109] At the same time, however, 60 members of the House, led by Congressman Theodore S. Weiss, urged Carter to stand firm on halting production of the neutron bomb. "We strongly support your decision and urge you to withstand the efforts to reverse it you will encounter in the coming days," a letter by these members of Congress said.[110]

In an effort to divert criticism and gain support for his decision, Carter met with members of the congressional leadership on April 15. "He said he would discuss it further with members of Congress before announcing his decision," House Democratic Leader Jim Wright told reporters.[111] But he added that "there was no discussion of the neutron bomb beyond the President's comment that he was considering it and was going to come to a position on it, but he wasn't there yet."[112] Even the president's supporters in Congress could not be rallied to his cause. Said a powerful Senate Democrat: "This has really hurt the President. It is the culmination of a series of disasters. There is deep concern here about the effects of this kind of aimless wandering on the conduct of substantive foreign policy."[113]

PACKAGING THE DECISION FOR PUBLIC CONSUMPTION

The final decision on deferral was concocted after Carter had canceled the weapon entirely. "That was Washington's attempt to rewrite history," commented one observer.[114] It was a compromise between external forces—Bonn and London—that Carter interpreted as offering insufficient support for production, and domestic pressures by Congress and the president's foreign policy advisors who demonstrated that support for production did indeed exist. From the two days of intensive discussion in the White House following Genscher's visit emerged a decision that tried to accommodate all the pressures, domestic and foreign, that had been building since the previous June. In the end, Carter "decided to defer production of

weapons with enhanced radiation effects" but simultaneously to keep open the option of deploying the weapons in the future unless the Soviet Union "shows restraint in its conventional and nuclear arms programs and force deployments affecting the security of the US and Western Europe."[115] In fact, the decision had nothing at all to do with "Soviet restraint," or even with the Soviets' propaganda campaign, but had everything to do with Washington's attempt to divert attention from what had become one of the Carter administration's worst foreign policy disasters. That Carter would want to address the issue of Soviet weapons developments was not, in essence, an attempt to rebuke the Soviets for their heated propaganda campaign. Rather, Carter wanted to silence congressional criticism that he was soft on defense. The administration felt it could at least partially salvage its damaged image among conservatives by somehow saying that this decision was not a favor to the Soviets, that the administration would reconsider and go ahead with deployment if the Russians did not show restraint.[116] The administration was trying to "package the decision for public consumption." As Halperin notes:

> In order to minimize public opposition Presidents will frequently explain and justify their decision in rhetoric which they believe will secure the maximum domestic political support for their proposal even if it does not precisely reflect the reasoning which leads them to the decision. They will seek an explanation that will draw the widest possible support and make it difficult for opposition groups to challenge them.[117]

If Carter did not envision reciprocal Soviet restraint, he also did not anticipate deploying the weapons in Europe during the remainder of his term in office. The decision to "defer production" was qualified by ordering the Defense Department "to proceed with the modernization of the Lance missile nuclear warhead and the 8-inch (artillery) weapons system, leaving open the option of installing the enhanced radiation element."[118] This statement was interpreted, and subsequently confirmed by the administration the following fall, to mean that all the components for an enhanced radiation warhead would be produced but that the warhead itself could not be entirely assembled without an executive directive. In military jargon, the new Lance missiles and artillery shells were "ER-convertible but not ER-capable." Although the White House claimed that modernization of the Lance missile and the 8-inch artillery shell would continue according to the original timetable,[119] the Defense Department knew that the political obstacles created by the controversy would, in reality, prevent deployment. "Any deferral in producing the missile warhead means a real delay no matter how you look at it," a Pentagon official said.[120] Some were even more skeptical, taking into account the magnitude of the political effort that would be required to reopen the issue. "After all the trouble this thing has caused," one official said, "do you think the White House

will want to go through it all over again in the near future? For all practical purposes, the neutron bomb is dead."[121] Now that the weapon was associated with Carter's ineffective leadership of the Alliance and with America's weakening commitment to the defense of Europe, to raise the issue again would seem only to confirm old suspicions.

Yet once the deferral decision had been announced, administration officials were compelled to justify it. Not only did it leave open the possibility of future production, they argued, but the Russians would have to be convinced that, if the United States did proceed, it would be only with the full understanding from the allies that the weapon would be deployed. By tying the decision to future Soviet restraint, the administration hoped to shift the onus of eventual production to Moscow. "If we do go to production and deployment in the future it will be quite clear to all political factions within the Western Alliance, and indeed to the entire world, that this decision . . . was only made in the presence of the failure on the part of the Soviet Union to show restraint in arms programs and deployments," said a White House defendant.[122] Finally, the administration wanted to believe that the debate had changed public attitudes about the neutron warhead: "The degree of public support, evidenced both in this country and abroad over the past few days, will make this weapon considerably more significant in any discussions or negotiations . . . with the Soviet Union about their arms programs and deployments which affect the security of the US and Western Europe."[123]

The president's critics both at home and abroad were not so easily mollified, however. To them the administration had appeared weak in this episode, the NATO alliance divided, and the future of its nuclear strategy uncertain. The European reaction to Carter's announcement reflected the belief that a pluralist approach to nuclear decision making was a dangerous, and ultimately disastrous, course for the Alliance. Making nuclear decisions within the forum of public opinion subjects the many formidable and often unanswerable questions about nuclear deterrence and defense to domestic pressures so persuasive that consensus is virtually impossible. European leaders know that when nuclear decisions are opened to public debate in their countries before NATO has reached agreement in private, they are unable to galvanize enough domestic support to make a convincing case for the decision on military grounds. The uncertainty surrounding the employment of nuclear weapons in Europe transformed private deliberation on substantive issues into public bickering over irrelevant emotional qualms and unrelated political issues.

If the purpose of an alliance is to defend itself against an external threat, the groups of sovereign nations who have come together for that reason must show common resolve toward that purpose. With this in mind, Bonn and London expressed modest support for Carter's decision despite their grave doubts about the supposed leader of the Alliance. "It is a signal for the other side to show their readiness for reduction or limitation of their growing

potential,"[124] Schmidt told Parliament. To satisfy his party's left wing, Schmidt attached "major significance" to the pursuit of arms control policies and stressed the continued need for NATO consultation on Alliance security requirements.[125] To satisfy his conservative critics, rebuff Moscow, and underscore Carter's decision as a temporary deferral, not definitive cancellation, Schmidt told Parliament he was ready to deploy the weapon in West Germany under two conditions: that NATO, as a whole, approve the weapon and that it be deployed with the forces of another continental nation.[126] To rebuild confidence in the Alliance he stressed that Bonn-Washington ties were as strong as ever: "German-American friendship is so strongly anchored that daily political differences of opinion, which can come up even in the best cooperation, cannot affect it."[127]

The British were even more positive in their public comments. Prime Minister Callaghan said the decision "rightly sets this matter in the context of arms control and the balance of forces on both sides."[128] Foreign Secretary Owen defended Carter's decision as "perfectly responsible and understandable" under the circumstances.[129]

Despite the outward appearance of satisfaction with the president's decision, Bonn and London had lost confidence in the president, both for the way the decision-making process was handled and for the event's implications for the future of European security. Not even opponents of the weapon indulged in unbounded glee at the strangely irrational way in which Washington handled the decision. The whole process struck Europe as sloppy, confused, and haphazard—unexplained and probably inexplicable. But who ever said decisionmaking was rational or easily explicable?

Europe's assessment is really not at all surprising, given what we know about how decisions were reached in Washington. American officials thought first of meeting their domestic and bureaucratic constraints, and only secondly of the processes internal to the foreign government they wished to influence. Policies devised in Washington were tailored to meet American needs first; thus the political strategy of reaching agreement on ERWs through an arms control framework was first of all a decision that seemed consistent with Washington politics. This strategy became Washington's accepted plan before any attempt was made to coordinate decisions with Bonn and London. Similarly, neither of Carter's decisions—to scrap the weapon entirely or to "defer" production—was based primarily on an assessment of what was needed to persuade the allies to endorse deployment. Carter's first decision reflects his own personal convictions and perhaps a fundamental ambivalence about neutron weapons. The final decision reflects the impact of bureaucratic constraints imposed by his foreign policy advisors and domestic pressures exerted by Congress. But neither were Schmidt's actions based on influencing Washington as much as they were directed at the German political scene. Pressures from both the left and right constrained Schmidt's actions, even though he personally favored deployment

of the weapon. Neustadt has noted that when one government "seeks to influence the conduct of another, everything depends upon the accuracy with which those who would wield influence perceive constraints impinging on the other"[130] government's behavior and apply what they perceive in their own actions. Unfortunately, these types of considerations were not the driving force behind the actions of the participants in the neutron bomb controversy.

NOTES

1. Michael Hornsby, "Brezhnev Says Neutron Bomb Threat to Detente," *Times* (London), January 24, 1978; "Letter by Brezhnev Warns NATO Lands on the Neutron Bomb," *Times*, January 24, 1978, p. A3; Vincent Ryder, "Brezhnev Warns 'Don't Accept N-Bomb,'" *Daily Telegraph* (London), January 24, 1978.

2. The message of Brezhnev's letter was reinforced in the United States the following week when the Kremlin-controlled World Peace Council held an anti-neutron "conference" in Washington on January 25. The Bureau of the World Peace Council Presidium demanded a ban on the neutron bomb and exhorted its members to mount a broad international campaign against the weapon. Several congressmen who had opposed appropriations for the weapons in September were invited to the first Washington rally of the Helsinki-based Council, though there is no record of any having attended. *Tass* in English, "The Washington Peace Proclamation and the Neutron Bomb," (EE/5727/A1/1), January 30, 1978; Rowland Evans and Robert Novak, "Behind the Neutron Decision," Washington *Post*, April 10, 1978.

3. Michael Hornsby, "NATO Anger at Brezhnev Letter on Neutron Bomb," *Times* (London), February 2, 1978.

4. Ibid.

5. Ibid.

6. John Hunt, "Neutron Bomb: PM Hits at Soviet Propaganda," *Financial Times*, February 22, 1978.

7. Jonathan Carr, "Bonn Resists Pressure over Neutron Weapons," *Financial Times* (London), February 23, 1978; Jean Wetz, "Les Sociaux–Democrates Temperent leur Opposition à la Bombe à Neutrons," *Le Monde* (Paris), February 24, 1978.

8. Carr, *Financial Times*, February 22, 1978.

9. Michael Getler, "Schmidt Calls for Talks on N-Bomb," *Guardian* (London), February 24, 1978; David Shears, "Germany Weighs Vital Interests on Neutron Bomb," *Daily Telegraph* (London), February 24, 1978.

10. Wetz, *Le Monde*, February 24, 1978.

11. Getler, Guardian (London), February 24, 1978.

12. Ibid.

13. Elizabeth Young, "Letter to the Editor," *Times* (London), March 1978.

14. Ibid.

15. Interview with Richard Burt, Washington, D.C., August 20, 1980.

16. Richard Burt, "Aides Report Carter Bans Neutron Bomb; Some Seek Reversal," New York *Times*, April 4, 1978, p. A4.

17. David Binder, "Ties with Bonn have Weakened, US Aides Say," New York *Times*, March 5, 1978, p. 6.

18. John Robinson, "US May Use Neutron Bomb as Tool in Arms Talks," *International Herald Tribune*, March 11, 1978.

19. Ibid.

20. Ibid.

21. "Soviet Bars Deal on Neutron Bomb," New York *Times*, March 12, 1978; p. 6.

22. Ibid.

23. Ibid.

24. "NATO to get Neutron Warhead," *Financial Times* (London), March 2, 1978; Reginald Dale, "US Set to Build Neutron Bomb," *Financial Times*, March 2, 1978; Clare Hollingworth, "Go-ahead on Neutron Bomb Likely if NATO Will Deploy It," *Daily Telegraph*, March 3, 1978.

25. Bernard Weinraub, "Haig Questioned on How Strongly Allies Back NATO," New York *Times*, March 2, 1978, p. A3.

26. "Dutch Against Neutron Bomb," *Financial Times*, February 24, 1978.

27. "Dutch Votes Bar N-Bomb Stand," *International Herald Tribune*, March 2, 1978.

28. Charles Batchelor, "Dutch Defense Minister Quits over Neutron Bomb," *Financial Times*, March 6, 1978.

29. "Neutron Bomb Opposed by Dutch Parliament," New York *Times*, March 9, 1978, p. A5.

30. Christopher Hitchens, "The Neutron Bomb and the Conscience of the Dutch," *New Statesman*, April 7, 1978, p. 455.

31. "The Hague Shuns a Commitment on Neutron Bomb," *International Herald Tribune*, March 9, 1978.

32. Ibid.

33. "Neutron Bomb Opposed by Dutch Parliament," New York *Times*, March 9, 1978, p. A5.

34. *International Herald Tribune*, March 9, 1978.

35. Richard Burt, "Neutron Bomb Controversy Strained Alliance and Caused Splits in the Administration," New York *Times*, April 9, 1978, p. 18.

36. "Furor over the Neutron Bomb," *Newsweek*, April 17, 1978, p. 38.

37. Ibid.

38. This official's perspective seems to reflect self-rationalization in retrospect of the aborted agreement. He could justify Carter's decision not to proceed with production and deployment by believing that, in spite of intensive consultations and negotiations, Schmidt remained uncommitted to the American formula. At the very least, he thought that Schmidt's alleged commitment was marked by vacillation and that signals from Bonn ran counter to private negotiations and the State Department's assessment of them.

39. "Carter Statement on Neutron Bomb," New York *Times*, April 8, 1978, p. A7.

40. Burt, "Neutron Bomb Controversy Strained Alliance," New York *Times*, April 9, 1978, p. 18.

41. "Furor over the Neutron Bomb," *Newsweek*, April 17, 1978, p. 39.

42. Ibid.

43. Burt, "Neutron Bomb Controversy Strained Alliance," New York *Times*, April 9, 1978, p. 18.

44. Ibid.

45. "Furor over the Neutron Bomb," Newsweek, April 17, 1978, pp. 35, 37.

46. Jimmy Carter, "Three Steps Toward Nuclear Responsibility," Bulletin of Atomic Scientists 32 (October 1976): 8-14.

47. See Chapter 4.

48. Flora Lewis, "NATO Officials Uneasy over Carter Administration's Foreign Policy," New York Times, April 1, 1978, p. A5.

49. Ibid.

50. "The Mishandled Bomb," New York Times, April 6, 1978, p. A20.

51. "Furor over the Neutron Bomb," Newsweek, April 17, 1978, p. 37.

52. Burt, "Neutron Bomb Controversy Strained Alliance," New York Times, April 9, 1978, p. A20.

53. "The Mishandled Bomb," New York Times, April 6, 1978, p. A20.

54. Interviews at ACDA, Defense Department, and State Department, Washington, D.C., August 1980.

55. Lewis, New York Times, April 1, 1978, p. A5.

56. Burt, "Neutron Bomb Controversy Strained Alliance," New York Times, April 9, 1978, p. 18.

57. General A. Haig, "The Military Case for the Neutron Warhead," Press Conference, Washington, D.C. March 21, 1978.

58. Burt, "Neutron Bomb Controversy Strained Alliance," New York Times, April 9, 1978, p. 18.

59. Richard Burt, "NATO Agreement on Neutron Bomb Expected Soon," New York Times, March 28, 1978, p. A7.

60. Terrence Smith, "The Maybe Bomb: Neutron Warhead has Political Fallout," New York Times, April 9, 1978, p. 1.

61. Clare Hollingworth, "NATO Delay in Neutron Bomb Talks," Daily Telegraph, March 22, 1978; Tony Geraghty and Reuben Ainsztein, "Why the West's New Bomb Is in Limbo," Sunday Times (London) March 26, 1978; Burt, "NATO Agreement on Neutron Expected Soon," p. A7; Walter Pincus, "US Pulls Back from NATO Neutron Weapons Discussions," Washington Post, March 28, 1978, p. 3.

62. "Furor over the Neutron Bomb," Newsweek, April 17, 1978, p. 38.

63. "The Neutron Bomb Furor," Time, April 17, 1978, p. 11.

64. Ibid.

65. "The Neutron Bomb Furor," p. 11; "The Neutron Mess," Sunday Times, April 9, 1978.

66. "Carter Has World Waiting on Neutron," International Herald Tribune, April 6, 1978, p. 2.

67. John Vincour, "US Gave a Hint to Bonn of Shift of Policy on Bomb," New York Times, April 5, 1978, p. A3.

68. Ibid.

69. "The Neutron Bomb Furor," Time, April 17, 1978.

70. On April 1 Christopher arrived in London to break the news to Foreign Secretary David Owen. Although Whitehall, unlike Bonn, was not appalled by the news, the British government thought that if Carter wanted to cancel the weapon, he should have done so nine months earlier, not when the Alliance was finally on the verge of tolerating deployment. While Prime Minister Callaghan was clearly perturbed, his

political stature was less affected by Carter's reversal than was a categorical decision that was, in any case, not its responsibility. Britain had throughout sought to play its customary role of "honest broker," contributing to the general discussion among NATO powers to reach a collective view. London agreed with Bonn that the weapon should not be deployed until some attempt had been made to obtain Soviet concessions in exchange. But Whitehall would have been willing to persuade Bonn to accept the weapon if Carter did decide to produce it. Moreover, London would supply the warheads for use by the British Army on the Rhine, if the president did go ahead. Henry Stanhope, "Britain Is Expected to Back Neutron Bomb," *Times* (London), April 4, 1978; "The Neutron Mess," Sunday *Times* (London), April 9, 1978.

71. Interview with Richard Burt, Washington, D.C., August 20, 1980.

72. "Furor over the Neutron Bomb," *Newsweek*, April 17, 1978, p. 35.

73. "The Neutron Bomb Furor," *Time*, April 17, 1978.

74. New York *Times*, April 4, 1978, p. A1.

75. Interview with Richard Burt, Washington, D.C., August 20, 1980.

76. Bernard Gwertzman, "Neutron Policy and Diplomacy," New York *Times*, April 4, 1978, p. A1.

77. Richard Burt, "Carter is Reported Reconsidering a Ban on the Neutron Bomb," New York *Times*, April 5, 1978, p. A1.

78. Richard Burt, "Pressure from Congress Mounts to Reverse Ban on Neutron Bomb," New York *Times*, April 6, 1978.

79. Burt, "Carter Is Reported Reconsidering," New York *Times*, April 5, 1978, p. A1.

80. David Cross, "Mr. Vance Confirms Decision Imminent on US Neutron Bomb," *Times* (London), April 5, 1978, p. 1.

81. "The Neutron Bomb Furor," *Time*, April 17, 1978.

82. Interview with Burt, August 20, 1980.

83. Ibid.

84. Burt, "Pressure from Congress Mounts," New York *Times*, April 6, 1978, p. A1.

85. Ibid.

86. Ibid, p. A9.

87. Ibid.

88. Ibid.

89. "The Neutron Mess," Sunday *Times*, April 9, 1978.

90. Richard E. Neustadt, *Alliance Politics* (New York: Columbia University Press, 1970), p. 140.

91. John Vincour, "Bonn Says Allied Alarm Caused Carter Weapons Shift," New York *Times*, April 6, 1978, p. A5.

92. Ibid.

93. "The Neutron Mess," Sunday *Times*, April 9, 1978.

94. Ibid.

95. "The Neutron Bomb Furor," *Time*, April 17, 1978.

96. "The Neutron Mess," Sunday *Times*, April 9, 1978.

97. "Carter Has World Waiting on Neutron," *International Herald Tribune*, April 6, 1978.

98. Richard Burt, "Neutron Bomb Controversy Strained Alliance," New York *Times*, April 9, 1978, p. 18.

99. Ibid.

100. Smith, New York *Times*, April 9, 1978, p. 1.

101. "Carter Has World Waiting on Neutron," *International Herald Tribune*, April 6, 1978.

102. Burt, "Neutron Bomb Controversy Strained Alliance," New York *Times*, April 9, 1978, p. 18.

103. Gwertzman, New York *Times*, April 5, 1978, p. A4.

104. "Furor over the Neutron Bomb," *Newsweek*, April 17, 1978, p. 39.

105. Ibid.

106. Burt, "Pressure from Congress Mounts," New York *Times*, April 6, 1978, p. A1.

107. Ibid.

108. Burt, "Carter is Reported Reconsidering," New York *Times*, April 5, 1978, p. A5.

109. Burt, "Pressure from Congress Mounts," New York *Times*, April 6, 1978, p. A1.

110. Ibid, p. A9.

111. "Carter has World Waiting on Neutron," *International Herald Tribune*, April 6, 1978.

112. Ibid.

113. "Furor over the Neutron Bomb," *Newsweek*, April 17, 1978, p. 39.

114. Interview with Burt, August 20, 1980.

115. "Carter Statement on Neutron Bomb," p. A7.

116. New York *Times* National Security Correspondent Richard Burt was, like many others, cynical about the outcome of the affair. He told me: "Occasionally when I see Jody Powell I ask him if the Soviets have exercised restraint!" Interview with Burt, August 20, 1980.

117. Morton Halperin, *Bureaucratic Politics and Foreign Policy* (Washington, D.C.: The Brookings Institution, 1974), p. 77.

118. "Carter Statement on Neutron Bomb," p. A7.

119. Hugh Muir, "Keeping an Option Open on the Neutron Warhead," *International Communications Agency* (London), April 10, 1978, p. 1.

120. Richard Burt, "President Decides to Defer Production of Neutron Weapons," New York *Times*, April 8, 1978, p. A7.

121. Ibid.

122. Hugh Muir, "Keeping an Option Open on the Neutron Warhead," ICA (London), April 10, 1978, p. 2.

123. Ibid.

124. "Schmidt Backs Neutron Delay," *International Herald Tribune*, April 14, 1978.

125. Ibid.

126. Ibid.

127. Ibid.

128. London Backs Carter Decision," New York *Times*, April 18, 1978, p. A6.

129. Henry Stanhope, "Dr. Owen Sees Carter Policy on Neutron Bomb as 'Responsible,' " *Times* (London), April 13, 1978.

130. Neustadt, p. 74.

7

Looking Ahead:
The Future of Tactical
Nuclear Weapons in NATO

The neutron bomb controversy is perhaps the most salient example in recent history of a breakdown in Alliance nuclear relations. It was a unique event in Alliance relations because the weapon itself hardly merited the transatlantic row it caused. As such, the consequences of the controversy go beyond the debate over the weapon itself. Its symbolic association with fundamental Alliance issues—of strategy, technology, and politics—is indicative of an evolutionary change in the broad strategic context on which Alliance security is based.

NATO's strategy of flexible response presupposes the existence of a credible U.S. strategic deterrent and of a relatively stable relationship between the United States and the Soviet Union. As the strategic relationship between the superpowers has changed over time, with the acquisition of new capabilities and the consequent change in the relative balance of forces, the foundation of NATO nuclear strategy has begun to erode. Allied governments now doubt the willingness of the United States to invoke the use of its strategic forces in the defense of Europe. This concern has created a climate in which Alliance members are likely to challenge the assumptions on which NATO strategy is based.

A combination of changes in the strategic environment in the last decade is slowly forcing a reconsideration of the validity of NATO's strategy of flexible response and the concepts of extended deterrence and forward defense that comprise it. First, the advent of parity between the United States and the Soviet Union has decreased the credibility of the American pledge to employ strategic nuclear forces in the event of Soviet aggression against Europe. Concern over developments in the nuclear capabilities of both superpowers

are indicative of a less stable strateic relationship between them. This condition has served to focus attention on the balance of forces at lower levels, specifically on battlefield nuclear forces. Second, general recognition within the Alliance that NATO's conventional forces are inadequate has increased concern that NATO might be forced to use battlefield nuclear weapons early in a conflict. Thus perceived inadequacies in both strategic and conventional forces have highlighted the role of tactical nuclear weapons in Alliance strategy and force posture. Finally, the general deterioration in East-West relations, economic and cultural as well as military, and the consequent heightening of public awareness about the dangers of nuclear war, have created an environment that is generally inhospitable for the modernization of tactical nuclear weapons.

It is within this broad context that the controversy over the neutron bomb must be viewed. That the weapon is at present not deployed in Europe is less important than the climate it has helped to create for a review of NATO's nuclear strategy. As a catalyst for provoking reconsideration of NATO doctrine and force posture, the neutron bomb controversy contains important lessons for future modifications of NATO's tactical nuclear stockpile. The following five propositions attempt to capture the major themes of the neutron bomb controversy within the franework of Alliance politics and strategy and to suggest how they apply to present and future nuclear issues in NATO.

1. *The bottom line of Alliance nuclear relations is not NATO's military doctrine but Europe's confidence in America's will.*

With the loss of American strategic superiority, Europe can no longer be certain of U.S. willingness to defend Europe with strategic nuclear forces. Thus the allies must now rely more heavily of U.S. intentions clarified through declaratory policy than on U.S. strategic nuclear capabilities. This condition makes Europe more sensitive to nuances of American policy, particularly to domestic debates about defense issues, that in the past.

NATO's nuclear strategy is shaped as much by the political processes between and within governments as by the context of external threat and perceptions of it. Institutional limitations, the presistence of excruciating domestic political problems in Europe, and the fragmentation of U.S. opinion and policy make doctrinal revision extremely risky. The political cohesion of the Alliance is often best preserved by avoiding extensive debate about NATO's nuclear strategy. Thus modernization that can be justified as improving NATO's ability to meet the requirements of current NATO strategy as codified in MC 14/3 is more acceptable than new capabilities that imply a change in present doctrine.

The neutron bomb controversy precipitated a heated doctrinal debate that broke the intellectual ice in Alliance nuclear relations. The outcome left NATO members with a feeling that the next modernization decision must

project the political cohesion of the Alliance. The ERW debacle helped to create the political will in Europe to support the deployment of cruise and Pershing missiles in December 1979. Having recognized the need to mobilize support for this decision after the divisive consequences of the neutron bomb controversy, the Alliance avoided doctrinal issues in order to reach agreement. However, the difficulties of solving political problems by nuclear remedies may ultimately undermine the political cohesion that the deployment of new nuclear missiles is intended to achieve.

2. *The political implications of deploying new nuclear weapons in Europe should be an integral part of the decision-making process.*

The principal lesson learned from the ERW fiasco was that domestic constraints on nuclear decisions must be addressed in a purposeful fashion if the Alliance is to avoid paralysis from within by domestic forces. Reflecting on the neutron bomb controversy, Carter administration officials noted that the failure of the allies to reach agreement on ERWs made Washington more sensitive to the future political management of nuclear decisions within NATO. American officials realized that the political dimensions of weapons modernization must be carefully worked through and made politically palatable to allied governments before consultation can proceed free from domestic obstructions. The ability of the allies to reach agreement on the deployment of cruise and Pershing missiles in 1979 was the direct result of the lessons learned from the chaotic management of the neutron bomb decision.

The ERW controversy was instrumental in exposing the inadequacies of NATO's consultative mechanisms, prompting the utilization of new institutional machinery to reach agreement on the deployment of intermediate range missiles. The so-called High Level Group (HLG) of NATO's Nuclear Planning Group has allowed senior defense officials from principal Alliance capitals to be an integral part of development of NATO nuclear policy, and a parallel Special Consultative Group (SCG) has been established to deal with arms control implications. Unlike the decision on intermediate-range missiles, the ERW case was not managed through NATO institutional structures. As a State Department official commented: "The NPG has a rigid structure which does not lend itself to subtle political discussions of the type necessary on this sensitive matter. NATO institutions didn't adapt well to the nuances of political give and take." Before the formation of the HLG, the United States had traditionally played a dominant role in the NPG in the development of Alliance nuclear policy. The United States initiated and directed procurement policy, while keeping the allies informed and consulting on deployment through the NPG. The HLG and SCG have facilitated a more prominent role for the Europeans on NATO nuclear issures. The participants in these recently established groups are representatives of their governments, rather than

NATO bureaucrats, allowing decisions to be lifted from the confines of the NATO bureaucracy. By enlarging the scope of consultation and the extent of intergovernmental communications, these consultative groups have enhanced the ability of the allies to reach agreement. Since 1979 the HLG and SCG have become the principal working-level forums for decisions on adjustments to NATO's nuclear stockpile and on approaches to European arms control, respectively.

3. Modernization of nuclear weapons in Europe cannot be managed by a pluralist approach to decision making.

Implicit in American policy with regard to the December 1979 decision on cruise and Pershing missiles was a desire to recoup the losses of what was considered a fiasco on nuclear matters within the Alliance in 1977-78. There was a strong sense that the United States had not shown leadership in the ERW controversy. As one American participant noted, "Washington learned from the neutron bomb that it could not, on a sensitive nuclear issue, merely tell its European allies that it was prepared to do what they wanted."[1] European leaders must be able to show their parliaments that the United States has made a firm commitment prior to allied consultations on deployment. Aware of its earlier mistakes, Washington left no doubt about its desired outcome on intermediate-range missiles; the allies followed America's lead.

The willingness of the allies to endorse the deployment of cruise and Pershing missiles was a direct result of their enhanced role in the early stages of decision making, as facilitated by the HLG and SCG. The rising domestic political costs of any adjustment to NATO's nuclear posture make it imperative that intraalliance disagreements be resolved in such private, working-level forums before the decision is presented to the public. Within such forums, the United States has, since the neutron bomb controversy, demonstrated a willingness to take the initiative on the nature of adjustments required.

In 1982 the HLG began a review of NATO's short- and medium-range nuclear weapons.[2] This study, in which all NATO members participate, is directed by the United States in its traditional role as nuclear guarantor of the Alliance. While the conclusions of this review will reflect an Alliancewide consensus, the United States will lead the effort by conducting the bulk of the analysis and providing Alliance members with options for adjustments to NATO's nuclear forces. The guidance provided by the U.S. government will facilitate the achievement of Alliance agreement on the future of NATO's nuclear forces, without the perils of a pluralist approach to decision making.

4. *The dual-track notion of parallel modernization and arms control has set a powerful precedent for future nuclear initiatives in NATO.*

The neutron bomb controversy institutionalized the role of arms control in allied decisions on the modernization of nuclear weapons in Europe. Arms control was used to further, rather than to abate, the deployment of neutron weapons. It has since become an indispensable feature of the decision to deploy intermediate-range missiles in Europe. This latter agreement was made conditional upon an attempt to limit the deployment of cruise and Pershing missiles through arms control negotiations in the four year interim between production starts and actual deployment. The 1979 decision has set a precedent that may allow European governments to refuse to deploy new nuclear weapons unless modernization is accompanied by arms control.

Using arms control as a political catalyst to expedite the decision making process and to sustain support for deployment in Europe, however, may very well pose huge obstacles to the future modernization of NATO's nuclear arsenal. The dual-track process has forced the Alliance into a spurious polemic in which the United States is accused of not being serious about arms control, and Europe is accused of not being committed to modernization. In a very real sense, arms control has become a "fig leaf" with which to conceal deep-seated differences within the Alliance. For the United States, arms control is important principally insofar as it produces militarily significant and adequately verifiable force reductions. For many allied leaders, however, arms control has become generally less important for its results than for its political symbolism as a process that ties the United States and Europe to the pursuit of a cooperative relationship with the Soviet Union. There is thus an inherent tension between the process and substance of arms control.

The Reagan administration would like to divorce the notion of concurrent modernization and arms control in future decisions on NATO's nuclear stockpile. The outcome of the HLG's current review of NATO's nuclear forces likely will not incorporate a dual-track approach; but the precedent set by the 1979 decision will probably require future modernization decisions to incorporate some compensating form of reductions. The analogous component of the arms control track of the 1979 decision may very well take the form of intra-alliance trade-offs on modernization and unilateral reductions such that the size of the current nuclear stockpile in Europe does not increase.[3] Given the increasing complexity and difficulty of arms control negotiations with the Soviet Union, modernization decisions accompanied by internal Alliance trade-offs may enhance the prospects of maintaining Alliance solidarity in a turbulent strategic environment.

5. *Future adjustments to NATO's tactical nuclear posture are likely to prompt an extensive review of the role of nuclear weapons in Europe.*

With the exception of the enhanced radiation warhead, NATO's tactical nuclear weapons have traditionally attracted much less popular attention than long-range theater nuclear forces. However, the inherent ambiguity in NATO doctrine about the potential use of battlefield nuclear weapons has been a constant source of debate in academic, government, and Alliance circles. From the outset of their deployment in the mid-1950s, Alliance members have differed over the employment plans for tactical nuclear weapons, and NATO doctrine has remained deliberately obscure. While the United States maintained strategic superiority over the Soviet Union, a limited nuclear war confined to Europe seemed extremely remote. Thus allied consensus on the need for TNW was possible, even though Alliance members did not agree on how and when they would be used in a conflict. The most general approach has been that NATO would use its TNW "as soon as necessary and as late as possible."[4]

Since the doctrinal debate precipitated by the neutron bomb controversy, however, a number of trends have converged, suggesting that NATO can no longer afford to ignore the ambiguities in its strategy for the selective employment of nuclear weapons. First, allied governments now feel an urgent need to respond to the growing antinuclear sentiment in both the United States and Europe. Many European governments would welcome a review of NATO's battlefield nuclear weapons that would suggest NATO could rationalize its posture by reducing the number of short-range systems deployed in Europe.[5] This would allow European governments, particularly the FRG, to present to their constituents compensating reductions in return for the deployment of cruise and Pershing missiles.

Second, many Alliance members are becoming increasingly aware that the present tactical nuclear systems are militarily ineffective, and therefore NATO has little to lose and much to gain, particularly in a political sense, from reductions accompanied by modernization of only part of the current force. Finally, the emergence of a number of technological developments suggests that conventional systems could potentially perform some missions currently filled by nuclear systems.

These pressures have made it inevitable that the Alliance now look at the tactical nuclear stockpile as a whole, not merely at the modernization of nuclear artillery with enhanced radiation warheads. In fact, the neutron bomb is deliberately excluded from the present discussions within NATO forums on the role of nuclear weapons in Europe. The issues raised in the present review, however, are similar to those prompted by the neutron bomb controversy: What is the relationship of tactical nuclear weapons to the nuclear threshold? Will the introduction of modernized nuclear systems make the prospect of early nuclear use more or less likely? But such questions are now posed in a broader context in which the explicit purpose of the HLG study is to review NATO's battlefield nuclear force posture, rather than merely to endorse the deployment of a new nuclear system.

The Reagan administration has appropriately put the neutron bomb on the back burner of Alliance nuclear issues; but this was not done without first testing European reaction: In August 1981 President Reagan announced his intention to complete production of enhanced radiation warheads for the 8-inch artillery shell and Lance missile. This unilateral decision did not reflect an understanding of European political constraints; on the contrary, the administration's attitude was that "the United States could not allow decisions on the military capabilities of its own forces to be dominated by European political concerns."[6] Chancellor Schmidt, clearly distraught by this attitude, responded that, among other conditions, his position on deployment in Europe would be linked to American demonstration of greater sensitivity to West European public opinion in making policy pronouncements. Schmidt also indicated that the conditions he had laid out in 1978—that the weapon must be deployed with the forces of at least one other continental ally, that deployment must be based on a joint NATO decision, and that arms control negotiations with the Soviet Union must have failed to produce positive results—were still applicable.[7] Thereafter discussion of deploying neutron warheads in Europe ceased, and they are presently stockpiled in the United States. Plans for deployment will remain dormant pending the outcome of cruise and Pershing deployments, which are considered too important to jeopardize with the introduction of neutron weapons. The neutron bomb is no longer an object of Soviet propaganda—ample evidence that the weapon is not currently on the agenda of NATO nuclear issues.

However, technological and bureaucratic imperatives make it unlikely that the neutron bomb will remain merely an historical footnote to the Carter presidency. Enhanced radiation warheads are militarily useless at their present storage sites in the United States, and they could not be transported to Europe in a crisis without the consent of the allies, which does not appear to be forthcoming. Powerful portions of the American defense community see a need for deployment of neutron warheads in Europe as soon as possible, but they are silenced by fear of disrupting cruise and Pershing deployments. Over the years, the neutron bomb has acquired a strong constituency in certain military circles. Such individuals are likely to advocate deployment in spite of the potential political risks within the Alliance.

The problem that decision makers face is distinguishing between bureaucratic and programmatic interest, combined with technological momentum, on the one hand, and Alliancewide objectives and allied political constraints, on the other. "Unfortunately, precedent suggests that the real lesson to be learned is that governments rarely learn lessons." New administrations come to Washington with the intention of correcting the mistakes of their predecessors. However, the mistakes they recognize are usually only those that can be extracted from *intra*governmental games, rather than those that require insight into *inter*Alliance politics. Thus the Reagan

administration saw a need to give the appearance of restoring American leadership within NATO—a lesson derived from politics in Washington; whether the present administration, or any other, can incorporate into its nuclear policies an awareness of the constraints impinging on allied governments' behavior—a lesson derived from Alliance politics—is uncertain. For many years the risks involved in the strategy of flexible response have been conveniently ignored. In the near future, facing the challenge of nuclear rearmament in Europe and the consequent fear of nuclear conflict, NATO will be obliged to explain and justify the ambiguities in its nuclear strategy. By the late 1980s, NATO may very well revisit the neutron bomb controversy.

NOTES

1. Gregory F. Treverton, "Global Threats and Trans-Atlantic Allies," *International Security* 5 (Fall 1980): 146.

2. U.S. Congress, Senate, *Second Interim Reported on Nuclear Weapons in Europe*, prepared by the North Atlantic Assembly's Special Committee on Nuclear Weapons in Europe, 98th Cong., 1st sess., January 1983.

3. Ibid.

4. Ibid, p. 7.

5. Ibid.

6. Leslie Gelb, "Reagan Reported to Order Building of Neutron Arms for Stockpiling in the U.S.," New York *Times*, August 9, 1981, p. 1.

7. "Schmidt Open to a Neutron Role," New York *Times*, August 25, 1981, p. 1.

BOOKS

Allison, Graham T. *Essence of Decision: Explaining the Cuban Missile Crisis.* Boston: Little, Brown, 1971.

Art, Robert J. *The TFX Decision: McNamara and the Military.* Boston: Little, Brown, 1968.

Atlantic Institute. *Dilemmas of the Atlantic Alliance: Two Germanys, Scandanavia, Canada, NATO and the EEC.* New York: Praeger, 1973.

Beaufre, Andre. *Deterrence and Strategy.* New York: Praeger, 1966.

Beer, Francis A., ed. *Alliances: Latent War Communities in the Contemporary World.* New York: Holt, Rinehart and Winston, 1970.

Booth, Ken. *Strategy and Ethnocentrism.* London: Croon Helm, 1979.

Clarke, Duncan L. *Politics of Arms Control: The Role and Effectiveness of the U.S. Arms Control and Disarmament Agency.* New York: Free Press, 1979.

Cohen, Sam. *The Truth About the Neutron Bomb: The Inventor of the Bomb Speaks Out.* New York: William Morrow, 1983.

Fox, William T. R. and Annette B. Fox. *NATO and the Range of American Choice.* New York: Columbia University Press, 1967.

Friedman, Julian R., Christopher Bladen, and Steven Rosen, eds. *Alliance in International Politics.* Boston: Allyn and Bacon, 1970.

Gatzke, Hans W. *Germany and the United States: A "Special Relationship?"* Cambridge, Mass.: Harvard University Press, 1980.

Halperin, Morton H. *Bureaucratic Politics and Foreign Policy,* Washington, D.C.: The Brookings Institution, 1974.

_____ . *Contemporary Military Strategy.* London: Faber and Faber, 1967.

_____ . *Defense Strategies for the Seventies.* Boston: Little, Brown, 1971.

Holst, Johan J. and Uwe Nerlich, eds. *Beyond Nuclear Deterrence: New Aims, New Arms.* London: Macdonald and Jane's, 1977.

Kissinger, Henry A. *The Troubled Partnership: A Re-appraisal of the Atlantic Alliance.* New York: Doubleday, 1966.

Morgan, Roger. *The United States and West Germany, 1945-1973: A Study in Alliance Politics.* London: Oxford University Press for the Royal Institute of International Affairs and the Harvard Center for International Affairs, 1974.

Neustadt, Richard E. *Alliance Politics.* New York: Columbia University Press, 1970.

_____ . *Presidential Power: The Politics of Leadership*. New York: John Wiley, 1968.

Neustadt, Richard E. *Alliance Politics*. New York: Columbia University Press, 1970.

Osgood, Robert Endicott. *NATO: The Entangling Alliance*. Chicago: University of Chicago Press, 1962.

Possony, Stefan T. and J. E. Pournelle. *The Strategy of Technology: Winning the Decisive War*. Cambridge, Mass.: Dunellen, 1970.

Record, Jeffery. *U.S. Nuclear Weapons in Europe: Issues and Alternatives*. Washington, D.C.: The Brookings Institution, 1974.

Richardson, James L. *Germany and the Atlantic Alliance: The Interaction of Strategy and Politics*. Cambridge, Mass.: Harvard University Press, 1966.

Schelling, Thomas C. *Arms and Influence*. New Haven, Conn.: Yale University Press, 1966.

_____ .*The Strategy of Conflict*. Cambridge, Mass.: Havard University Press, 1960.

Schmidt, Helmut. *Defense or Retaliation: A German View*. New York: Praeger, 1962.

Snyder, Glenn H. *Deterrence and Defense: Toward a Theory of National Security*. Princeton, N.J.: Princeton University Press, 1961.

Steinbrunner, John D. *The Cybernetic Theory of Decision: New Dimensions of Political Analysis*. Princeton, N.J.: Princeton University Press, 1974.

Stockholm International Peace Research Institute. *Tactical Nuclear Weapons: European Perspectives*. London: Taylor and Francis, 1978.

Talbott, Strobe, *Endgame: The Inside Story of SALT II*. New York: Harper and Row, 1979.

Thompson, James Clay. *Rolling Thunder: Understanding Policy and Program Failure*. Chapel Hill: University of North Carolina Press, 1980.

ARTICLES

Alford, Jonathan. "The Neutron Bomb." *Command*, November-December 1978, pp. 43-46.

Bennett, W. S., R. R. Sandoval, and R. G. Schreffler. "A Credible Nuclear–Emphasis Defense for NATO." *Orbis* 17 (Summer 1973): 463-79.

Bertram, Christoph. "European Security and the German Problem." *International Security* 4 (Winter 1979-80): 105-16.

Black, Edwin F. and S. T. Cohen. "The Neutron Bomb and the Defense of NATO." *Military Review*, May 1978, pp. 53-57.

Bracken, Paul. "Collateral Damage and Theatre Warfare." *Survival* 22 (September/October 1980): 203-7.

Brauch, Hans Gunther. "The Enhanced Radiation Warhead: A West German Perspective." *Arms Control Today* 8 (June 1978): 1-4.

Brenner, Michael J. "Tactical Nuclear Strategy and European Defense: A Critical Reappraisal." *International Affairs*, no. 1 (1975), pp. 23-42.

Burt, Richard. "Reassessing the Strategic Balance." *International Security* 5 (Summer 1980): 37-52.

Center for Defense Information. "NATO and the Neutron Bomb." *The Defense Monitor* 7 (June 1978): 1-8.

Cohen, S. T. "Enhanced Radiation Warheads: Setting the Record Straight." *Strategic Review* 6 (Winter 1978): 9-17.

Cohen, S. T. and W. R. Van Cleave. "Western European Collateral Damage from Tactical Nuclear Weapons." *Journal of the Royal United Services Institute of Defense Studies (RUSI)* June 1976, pp. 32-38.

Collins, Arthur S., Jr. "The Enhanced Radiation Warhead: A Military Perspective," *Arms Control Today* 8 (June 1978): 1-5.

Drell, Sidney D. and Frank von Hippel. "Limited Nuclear War." *Scientific American* 235 (November 1976): 2-12.

Ellsberg, Daniel. "There Must Be No Neutron Bomb." *Nation*, May 27, 1978, pp. 623-33.

Freedman, Lawrence. "The Dilemma of Theatre Nuclear Arms Control." *Survival* 23 (January/February 1981): 2-10.

Frye, Alton. "Slow Fuse on the Neutron Bomb." *Foreign Policy*, Summer 1978, pp. 95-103.

Geneste, M. "La 'Bombe à Neutrons,' la Défense de l'Europe et la 'Flexible Response.'" *Défense Nationale* 33 (December 1977): 43-57.

Gray, Colin S. "Theater Nuclear Weapons: Doctrines and Postures." *World Politics* 28 (January 1976): 300-14.

Hitchens, Christopher. "The Neutron Bomb and the Conscience of the Dutch." *New Statesman*, April 7, 1978, pp. 453-56.

Kaplan, Fred M. "Enhanced-Radiation Weapons." *Scientific American* 238 (May 1978): 44-51.

Kielmannsegg, J. A. Graf. "A German View of Western Defense." *Journal of the Royal United Services Institute for Defense Studies (RUSI)*. March 1974, pp. 11-18.

Kistiakowsky, George B. "Enhanced Radiation Warheads, Alias the Neutron Bomb." *Technology Review*, May 1978, pp. 24-30.

Komer, Robert. "Looking Ahead." *International Security* 4 (Summer 1979): 108-16.

Lewis, Kevin. "The Prompt and Delayed Effects of Nuclear War." *Scientific American* 241 (July 1979): 27-39.

Menaul, Stewart W. B. "The Military Balance and its Implications: A European View." *Strategic Review*, Summer 1977, pp. 47-57.

Merkl, Peter H. "Politico-Cultural Restraints on West German Foreign Policy: Sense of Trust, Identity, and Agency." *Comparative Political Studies*, January 1971, pp. 443-57.

Miettinen, Jorna K. "Enhanced Radiation Warfare." *Bulletin of Atomic Scientists* 33 (September 1977): 32-37.

Morgan, Roger. "Washington and Bonn: A Case Study in Alliance Politics." *International Affairs* 47 (July 1971): 489-502.

Pipes, Richard. "Why the Soviet Union Thinks It Could Fight and Win a Nuclear War." *Commentary*, July 1977, pp. 21-34.

Possony, Stefan T. "NATO and the Dawn of New Technology." *Defense and Foreign Affairs*, October 1976, pp. 15-18 and November 1976, pp. 18-20.

Robinson, J. P. Perry. "Neutron Bomb and Conventional Weapons of Mass Destruction." *Bulletin of Atomic Scientists*, March 1978, pp. 42-45.

Schmidt, Helmut. "Address for the 1977 Alastari Buchan Memorial Lecture." *Survival* 20 (January/February 1978).

Schreffler, R. G. "The Neutron Bomb for NATO Defense: An Alternative." *Orbis* 22 (Winter 1978): 959-973.

Sinnreich, Richard Hart. "NATO's Doctrinal Dilemma." *Orbis* 19 (Summer 1975): 461-76.

Sommer, Theo. The Neutron Bomb: Nuclear War Without Tears?" *Survival* 19 (November/December 1977): 263-66.

Treverton, Gregory F. "Global Threats and Trans-Atlantic Allies." *International Security* 5 (Fall 1980): 142-58.

Ulsamer, Edgar. "NATO: On the Road Toward A 'Coalition Warfare' Posture." *Air Force Magazine*, January 1978, pp. 50-56.

_____ ."The 'Neutron Bomb' Media Event." *Air Force Magazine*, November 1977, pp. 66-73.

Vardamis, Alex A. "German-American Military Fissures." *Foreign Policy* 34 (Spring 1979): 87-106.

_____ ."The Neutron Warhead: Stormy Past, Uncertain Future." *Parameters, Journal of the US Army War College* 8 (March 1978): 40-48.

Witze, Claude. "The Wayward Press: Fallout From the Neutron Bomb." *Air Force Magazine* 60 (November 1977): 20-21.

Worner, Manfred. "NATO Defense and Tactical Nuclear Weapons." *Strategic Review*, Fall 1977, pp. 11-18.

U.S. GOVERNMENT DOCUMENTS AND PUBLICATIONS
(in chronological order)

U.S. Congress. Senate. Senator Dodd speaking on the Nuclear Test-Ban Negotiations. February 21, March 7, and April 9, 1963. *Congressional Record*, pp. 2903-6, 3630-34, and 5985-90.

U.S. Congress. Joint Committee on Atomic Energy. *To Consider NATO Matters. Hearings before the Joint Committee on Atomic Energy*, 93rd Cong., 2nd sess., 1974.

U.S. Congress. Joint Committee on Atomic Energy. *The Consideration of Military Applications of Nuclear Technology. Hearings before the Subcommittee on Military Applications of the Joint Committee on Atomic Energy*, 93rd Cong., 1st sess., 1973.

U.S. Congress. Senate. Committee on Foreign Relations. *U.S. Nuclear Weapons in Europe and U.S.-U.S.S.R. Strategic Doctrines and Policies. Hearings before subcommittees of the Senate Committee on Foreign Relations.*, 93rd Cong., 2nd sess., 1974.

U.S. Congress. Senate. Committee on Foreign Relations. *U.S. Security Issues in Europe: Burden Sharing and Offset, MBFR, and Nuclear Weapons,* by James G. Lowenstein and Richard M. Moose. Washington, D.C.: U.S. Government Printing Office, 1973.

U.S. Congress. *The Theater Nuclear Force Posture in Europe. A Report to the United States Congress,* by James R. Schlesinger. Washington, D.C.: U.S. Government Printing Office, 1975.

U.S. Congress. Congressional Budget Office. *Planning U.S. General Purpose Forces: The Theater Nuclear Forces.* Washington, D.C.: U.S. Government Printing Office, 1977.

U.S. Congress. Senate. Committee on Armed Services. *NATO and the New Soviet Threat,* by Senators Sam Nunn and Dewey F. Bartlett. 95th Cong., 1st sess., Washington, D.C.: U.S. Government Printing Office, 1977.

U.S. Congress. House. Committee on Armed Services. *ERDA Authorization Legislation (National Security Programs) for Fiscal Year 1978. Hearings before a subcommittee of the House Committee on Armed Services on H.R. 6566,* 95th Cong., 1st sess., 1977.

U.S. Congress. Senate. Amendment of the Public Works Appropriation (The Neutron Bomb Debate). 95th Cong., 1st sess., July 1, and July 13, 1977. *Congressional Record,* pp. S11427-442. and S11741-789.

U.S. Congress. House. ERDA Authorizations for National Security Programs, Fiscal Year 1978 (The Neutron Bomb Debate). 95th Cong., 1st sess., September 13, 19, and 20, 1977. *Congressional Record,* pp. H9308-15, H9644-48 and E5733-34.

U.S. Congress. House. Committee on International Relations. *Additional Arms Control Impact Statement and Evaluations for Fiscal Year 1978.* 95th Cong., 1st sess., Washington, D.C.: U.S. Government Printing Office, 1977.

U.S. Congress. Senate. Committee on Armed Services. *Department of Defense Authorization for Appropriations for Fiscal Year 1979. Hearings before the Senate Committee on Armed Services on S. 2571.* 95th Cong., 2nd sess., pt. 9, 1978.

NEWSPAPERS

Daily Telegraph (London), June 6, 1977-April 30, 1978.
Financial Times (London), June 6, 1977-April 30, 1978.
Guardian (London), June 6, 1977-April 30, 1978.
International Herald Tribune, June 6, 1977-April 30, 1978.
New York *Times,* June 6, 1977-April 30, 1978.
Times (London), June 6, 1977-April 30, 1978.
Washington *Post,* June 6, 1977-April 30, 1978.

UNPUBLISHED MATERIALS

Leitenberg, Milton. "Some Major Points Regarding Enhanced Radiation Warheads, The 'Neutron Bomb,' and Related Issues." Hamburg, West Germany, 1978.

Nerlich, Uwe. "The Modernization of NATO's Theater Nuclear Forces: Some European Policy Constraints." London, 1976.

INTERVIEWS

Alford, Jonathan. International Institute for Strategic Studies, London. July, 10, 1980.

Ball, Desmond. International Institute for Strategic Studies, London. July 18, 1980.

Burt, Richard. New York *Times*, Washington, D.C. August 1980.

Cook, Robin. Labour Member of Parliament for Edinborough Central, London. July 24, 1980.

Freedman, Lawrence. Royal Insititute for International Affairs, London July 22, 1980

Pincus, Walter. Washington *Post*, Washington, D.C. August 15, 1980.

Roper, John. Labour Member of Parliament for Farnworth, London. July 24, 1980.

Stanhope, Henry. *Times* (London). July 18, 1980.

U.K. Ministry of Defence, London. July 1980.

U.S. Arms Control and Disarmament Agency, Washington, D.C. August 1980.

U.S. Department of Defense, Washington, D.C. August 1980.

U.S. Department of State, Washington, D.C. August 1980.

U.S. National Security Council, Washington, D.C. August 1980.

Windsor, Philip. London School of Economic and Political Science July 17, 1980.

Index

About the Author

SHERRI L. WASSERMAN grew up in Scarsdale, New York. She received her education at the London School of Economics and Amherst College, where she graduated *summa cum laude* for her thesis on *The Neutron Bomb Controversy*. While a student, she worked at the North Atlantic Assembly, NATO's interparliamentary body, and at the International Institute for Strategic Studies in London. She spent two years as a defense analyst with Science Applications, Inc., where she was a member of the team supporting the Department of Defense on NATO's review of nuclear weapons in Europe. Currently she is a student at Harvard Law School and the John F. Kennedy School of Government.